English Porcelain; a Handbook to the China Made in England During the Eighteenth Century as Illustrated by Specimens Chiefly in the National Collections

SOUTH KENSINGTON MUSEUM ART HANDBOOKS.

ENGLISH PORCELAIN.

ENGLISH PORCELAIN

A HANDBOOK TO THE CHINA MADE IN
ENGLAND DURING THE EIGHTEENTH
CENTURY AS ILLUSTRATED
BY SPECIMENS CHIEFLY
IN THE NATIONAL
COLLECTIONS.

BY

A. H. CHURCH,

M.A., F.R.S., PROFESSOR
OF CHEMISTRY IN THE ROYAL
ACADEMY OF ARTS IN LONDON.

WITH NUMEROUS WOODCUTS.

Published for the Committee of Council on Education
BY
CHAPMAN AND HALL, LIMITED, LONDON.

RICHARD CLAY AND SONS, LIMITED,
LONDON AND BUNGAY.

CONTENTS.

LIST OF ILLUSTRATIONS VII

PREFACE IX

BIBLIOGRAPHICAL NOTES XV

CHAPTER I.
HISTORICAL INTRODUCTION.

Porcelain invented in China—Imitated in Italy, Saxony, Austria, France, and England—Natural and Artificial Porcelain—Hard and Soft Paste—Materials and Classification 1

CHAPTER II.
CHELSEA.

Origin of the Chelsea Works—Gouyn and Sprimont—Auction Sales—First Period—Second Period—Derby-Chelsea—Chief Productions—Marks 14

CHAPTER III.
BOW.

Early History—Introduction of Bone-ash into the China-body—Characteristic Productions—Marks 26

CONTENTS.

CHAPTER IV.
DERBY

Origin—Duesbury—Bloor—Crown-Derby—Marks—Biscuit Figures . 35

CHAPTER V.
WORCESTER.

Wall and Davis, inventors of Worcester China—Changes of Ownership—Under- and Over-glaze Printing—Vases—Marks—Materials . . 43

CHAPTER VI.
PLYMOUTH.

Cookworthy discovers China-clay and China-stone—His Patent—Short duration of Works—Marks 56

CHAPTER VII.
BRISTOL.

Champion's Works — Advertisements and Auctions — Apprentices—Champion and Wedgwood—Choice Specimens—Marks 62

CHAPTER VIII.
STAFFORDSHIRE PORCELAIN

Longton Hall—New Hall—Davenport—Minton—Spode—Wedgwood . 73

CHAPTER IX.
MISCELLANEOUS PORCELAINS.

Lowestoft — Liverpool — Brancas-Lauraguais — Caughley — Coalport—Pinxton—Church-Gresley—Rockingham—Nantgarw—Swansea . . 81

LIST OF ILLUSTRATIONS.

S C.—Schreiber Collection   M P G —Museum Practical Geology   S K M —South Kensington Museum.   H F C —Mr. H F. Church.   J E N —Mr J E. Nightingale.

FIG		COLLECTION.	TO FACE PAGE
1.—Chelsea	Scent-bottle, "Dancing Lady"	S.C.	14
2.—Chelsea	Snuff-box in form of a head	S.C.	14
3.—Chelsea:	Snuff-box; Cupid and Drums	S C.	16
4.—Chelsea:	Chinese figure; early period	H F.C.	18
5.—Chelsea:	Leaf-shaped dish	M P.G.	18
6.—Chelsea:	Vase, Rococo style	S.K M.	20
7.—Chelsea:	Figure, "Fifer"	S C.	22
8.—Chelsea:	Figure, "Drummer"	S.C.	22
9.—Chelsea:	Vase, heart-shaped	S.K.M.	22
10.—Chelsea-Derby:	The Coopers' Bowl	S C.	22
11.—Chelsea-Derby:	Vase with biscuit handles	S.K.M.	24
12.—Chelsea-Derby:	Covered bowl and stand	S.C.	24
13.—Chelsea:	The Music Lesson	S.C.	24
14.—Chelsea:	Lord Chatham	S C.	24
15.—Bow:	Soup-tureen, white	S K.M	26
16.—Bow:	Dessert-dish, scallop shell	M.P.G.	26
17.—Bow:	Sauce-boat with blue painting	M.P.G.	30
18.—Bow:	Plate with birds and festoons	S.C.	30
19.—Bow:	Britannia, with medallion of George II.	S C	32
20.—Bow:	Vase, with wreaths and masks	S C	32
21.—Derby:	Statuette, Girl with lamb	S.C.	40
22.—Derby:	Statuette, Boy with dog	S C.	40
23.—Derby:	Statuette in biscuit, Diana	M.P.G.	40
24.—Derby:	Covered cup and saucer	M.P.G.	42
25.—Derby:	Plate with Amorino	M.P.G.	42

LIST OF ILLUSTRATIONS

FIG.		COLLECTION	TO FACE PAGE
26.—Derby: Coffee-can, with flowers		M P G.	42
27.—Worcester: Coffee-cup, blue printed		S K M	46
28.—Worcester: Mug, transfer over-glaze print		S C.	46
29.—Worcester: Vase, yellow ground, painted and printed		S.C.	48
30.—Worcester: Vase, painted with tropical birds		S C.	48
31.—Worcester: Tea-jar, enamelled and gilt		M P G	50
32.—Worcester: Centre-piece, shell work		J E N	50
33.—Worcester: Tea-cup, embossed pattern		A H C.	52
34.—Worcester: Bowl of tobacco-pipe		S C.	52
35.—Plymouth: Salt-cellar, white		M P G.	56
36.—Plymouth: Statuette, Asia		S.C.	58
37.—Plymouth: Statuette, America		S C.	60
38.—Bristol: Statuette, Winter		S C	66
39.—Bristol: Statuette, Boy with hurdy-gurdy		S C.	68
40.—Bristol: Statuette, Girl with triangle		S C	68
41.—Bristol: Vase, painted with trees and birds		S.C.	70
42.—Bristol: Tea-pot, rich blue ground		S.C.	70
43.—Bristol: Covered basket and stand		M P G.	72
44.—Longton Hall: Vase, with rim of flowers		A H C.	74
45.—Minton: Bowl, with flowers in panels		S K M.	78
46.—Caughley: Sugar-bason and cover		M.P.G.	88
47.—Pinxton: Ice-pail, with floral border		S K M.	90
48.—Nantgarw: Saucer, birds in panels		S K M.	92
49.—Swansea: Coffee-can, with groups of flowers		S.K.M	94

PREFACE.

In the "Handbook of English Earthenware" I nominally closed my account with the year 1800, but I began it with a notice of the sepulchral vessels made in England before the dawn of our National History. If the tale of English China to be outlined in the pages that follow were to be strictly limited to the time between the first manufacture of porcelain in this country and the end of the last century, it would embrace hardly more than fifty years. There are, however, several reasons why we should extend our discussion of English Porcelain beyond these narrow limits. Some of the famous factories of the last century have survived, not only so far as the beginning of the present century, but even to the present day. And between the years 1800 and 1820 or 1830 not a few new works were started, the productions of which were either closely connected with previous manufactures, or were marked by peculiarities of some importance in the history of Ceramic development Specimens of the china made at most of these later works are commonly included in collections of so-called "Old English" wares, and collectors will expect to find a notice of them in a handbook having the title given to that now in the hands of the reader.

I have discussed separately, in a few chapters of considerable length, the chief and earliest china factories of England, leaving a score or more of the lesser, and, for the most part, later, works to be described together in a couple of groups. But it is not possible to secure, in all cases, an adequate description of each fabrique—a description proportional to its importance. For instance, the factories of Bow and Chelsea having never been made the subjects of exhaustive research, our knowledge of their history remains fragmentary. But the case is different with the works at Derby, Worcester, and Bristol, which have been made the subjects of excellent monographs, for which we are indebted to Mr. John Haslem, Mr. R. W. Binns, and Mr. Hugh Owen, respectively. Of the smaller and more obscure factories we may learn much in some instances, very little in others. When a few thousand pounds have been sunk in a vain attempt at china-making, the circumstances of the failure are not willingly published far and wide. On the other hand, some of the minor factories have left tangible and fairly complete records of their history.

The origin and nature of English porcelain is treated with some fulness in my introductory chapter. I need not here recapitulate the distinctions between "hard" and "soft" paste, and between "natural" and "artificial" porcelain. These distinctions are dwelt upon in the earlier chapters of this handbook, where also will be found brief accounts of the chief materials employed in the several factories. For fuller details of a technical kind, and for more numerous analyses of clays and porcelains, reference may be made to some of the books named in my Bibliographical Notes.

In the Preface to the "Handbook of English Earthenware" (*p. xii*), I have spoken of the artistic decadence which set in towards the close of the eighteenth century. This decadence is perhaps even more marked in the case of porcelain than in that of earthenware. The lavish expenditure of all the resources of the enameller and the gilder upon the more costly china made between the years 1790 and 1850, was at once a sign and a cause of the prevalent loss of artistic feeling Art was smothered in artifice. Miracles of ceramic ingenuity were accomplished. Baskets, for example, were first built up, with great toil and painful care, of slender porcelain threads, and then the precarious structures were further decorated with sprays of flowers and foliage in "ronde bosse": the resulting marvel could scarcely be touched without suffering damage. In other cases the porcelain-body was so covered with matt and burnished gold, or with masses of finely painted and richly coloured flowers, that the nature of the ground could nowhere be recognised. The lavish ornament was no longer "en rapport" with the material, the use and the form of the vessels. The shapes, too, were often either ungainly or extravagant, all sense of temperance *of line being as thoroughly lost as was the feeling for reserve in colour. While signalizing these defects of many English porcelains, especially those of late date, it would be unfair to omit all reference to their merits. In the chapters devoted to Chelsea and Worcester I have more particularly endeavoured to do justice to the peculiar excellences of body and decoration which the productions of these factories so often exhibit. Its bizarre and rococo style may be regretted, but the technical merits of English porcelain are capable of teaching many useful lessons, and are of great value in the history of ornamental art.*

The illustrations in this Handbook have been drawn from selected, and, it is hoped, typical specimens of the several factories described. A statuette, a vase, and a cup, mug, plate, dish, bowl, or basket, belonging to each of the more important china works, have been figured. In the case of the less important, the less interesting, and the later manufactures, I have limited myself to half a dozen woodcuts, all told. This restriction will not, I think, be regretted, if the three following considerations be kept in mind. First, the majority of the productions of the above-mentioned works are characterized by a strong family likeness; or, second, they show qualities of paste or gilding, or sumptuous painting which cannot be adequately rendered by a woodcut; or, third, the forms which they assume are by no means pleasant to a trained eye. I felt, therefore, to cite one example, that a single specimen of early Minton porcelain would suffice to represent a whole group of factories, including those carried on by Davenport, Spode, and Wedgwood—so far, at least, as their productions in porcelain are concerned.

It is difficult to acknowledge adequately my obligations to previous writers and workers on English porcelain. The present small volume owes a great deal to the authors named in my Bibliographical Notes, and a great deal also to the kindness of the friends whose help I have acknowledged in the companion handbook on Earthenware. Amongst such friends I am bound to name once more the Lady Charlotte Schreiber, Dr. H. W. Diamond, Mr. J E. Nightingale, and Mr. H. Willett. My own work has been chiefly that of selection and arrangement. Here and there, however, I have added new facts, and helped to settle doubtful matters by careful study of collections of English china, and by chemical and microscopical analysis of individual specimens.

A. H. C.

13th January, 1885.

Since this Handbook was written much additional information has been placed at the disposal of students by Mr. W. Turner in his treatise on the productions of Swansea and Nantgarw, and by Mr. W. Bemrose in his volume relating chiefly to Derby porcelain. From these sources a few corrections have been introduced in the present issue of " English Porcelain "

The Schreiber Collection, so often mentioned in these pages, is now in the South Kensington Museum. the ownership of other specimens named has changed. And a note of mourning must be struck, for many of the author's friends amongst connoisseurs of English porcelain have passed away. We can no longer draw upon the abundant knowledge and kindly aid of The Lady Charlotte Schreiber, Dr. H W Diamond, Mr J E Nightingale, Sir A. Wollaston Franks, Mr. Hugh Owen, and Mr Wm Edkins.

A. H. C.

20th April, 1898

BIBLIOGRAPHICAL NOTES.

	YEAR
BINNS, R. W.—A Century of Potting in the City of Worcester, 2nd ed.	1877
BINNS, R. W.—Guide through the Worcester Royal Porcelain Works	1880
CHAFFERS, W.—Marks and Monograms on Pottery and Porcelain	1876
CHURCH, A. H.—Scientific and Artistic Aspects of Pottery and Porcelain; Cantor Lectures	1881
DAVILLIER, BARON C.—Origines de la Porcelaine en Europe	1882
FORTNUM, C. D. E., and others—Report on Pottery, London International Exhibition, 1871	1871
FRANKS, A. W.—Catalogue of Specimens of Oriental Porcelain	
HASLEM, J.—The Old Derby China Factory	1876
JEWITT, LL.—Ceramic Art in Great Britain	1878
MARRYAT, J.—History of Pottery and Porcelain, 3rd ed	1868
NIGHTINGALE, J. E.—Contributions towards the History of Early English Porcelain	1881
OWEN, H.—Two Centuries of Ceramic Art in Bristol	1873
REEKS, T., and RUDLER, F. W.—Catalogue of Specimens of English Pottery in the Museum of Practical Geology, 3rd ed.	1876
SODEN-SMITH, R. H.—Catalogue of English Pottery and Porcelain, Alexandra Palace	1873
TIFFIN, W. F.—A Chronograph of the Bow, Chelsea and Derby China Factories	1874

	YEAR
TURNER, WILLIAM.—The Ceramics of Swansea and Nantgarw	1897
BEMROSE, WILLIAM.—Bow, Chelsea and Derby Porcelain	1898

ENGLISH PORCELAIN.

CHAPTER I.

HISTORICAL INTRODUCTION.

Porcelain invented in China—Imitated in Italy, Saxony, Austria, France, and England.

THE word "porcelain" is of European origin, derived, in all likelihood, from the Italian *porcellana*, the name of the cowrie shell. The resemblance of the glazed surface of porcelain to that of this shell suggested the use of the word, while *porcellana* itself was a derivative of the Italian word *porcella*, a small pig, the cowrie shell having something of the form of that animal.

Although there is no doubt that porcelain was invented in China, there is much doubt concerning the date of its invention. Not only are the early Chinese records largely tinged with the romantic element, but the language used concerning ceramic wares is often obscure, the distinctions between earthenware, stoneware, and porcelain being frequently ill-defined or not defined at all. But it is now generally admitted that porcelain was first made during the Han dynasty, between 206 B.C. and A.D. 87. The development of the manufacture was at first slow, and the colours and decorations limited and simple. Under the Ming dynasty, 1368-1644, porcelain reached its highest perfection, although not until the reign of the second emperor (1661-1722) o the succeeding Tsing dynasty was the number of colours used much extended. Further advances in this direction were made during the reign of Keen-lung, 1736-1795.

The first distinct reference to porcelain out of China has been traced to the year 1171, when the Sultan Saladin sent forty pieces of Chinese porcelain to the Shah Nur-ed-din. Marco Polo visited in 1280 one of the places where porcelain was made, and mentions that it was exported all over the world; many notices from travellers of the fourteenth and fifteenth centuries might be adduced. Perhaps Chinese porcelain reached Europe through Egypt; at any rate a present of porcelain vases was sent in 1487 to Lorenzo de' Medici by the Sultan of Egypt. This fact is particularly interesting in connection with the earliest known manufacture of porcelain in Europe, namely, in 1575-1580 at Florence. It is doubtless to the Portuguese that Europe owes the first direct importation of porcelain from China; the Portuguese were followed by the "India Companies" of Holland, England, and France. Many beautiful old specimens of Chinese porcelain mounted in silver-gilt of European workmanship are extant; some of the mounts of the pieces which have blue decorations or celadon and turquoise glazes are English, and belong to the sixteenth century.

The successful imitation or reproduction of Chinese porcelain in Europe was dependent upon the discovery of its two essential ingredients, china-clay and china-stone. Much, however, of the most highly esteemed porcelain of Europe is not formed from these two materials, but from substances more or less allied to them in chemical composition, or which answer the same purposes. Thus, many of the white, or nearly white, clays which have been used from time to time in English and continental porcelains, contain chemical compounds almost if not quite identical with the hydrated silicate of alumina, which forms nearly the entire mass of true china-clay or kaolin, while the felspathic ingredient is also present in some of them.

So, too, the bone-ash and the soapstone, which have been so

largely used in English soft porcelains, may be regarded as fulfilling many of the functions of the original ingredients of true oriental hard porcelain. Before proceeding further with our account of the history of porcelain-making in Europe, and especially in England, it is desirable to explain briefly the nature of the fundamental and accessory materials employed in the manufacture.

Beginning with kaolin or china-clay (which has been called the bones of china, as china-stone or pe-tun-tse, its flesh), it should be stated that this forms the infusible or "refractory" part of porcelain It was named *marga porcellana* by the Swedish mineralogist, Wallerius, in 1747; in 1758 Cronstedt described it as *terra porcellanea*. It is the result of the alteration of many minerals containing alumina, notably of the felspars. Some specimens, the purest, contain, in 100 parts, 46 parts of silica, 39½ of alumina, 14 of water, and but ½ a part of magnesia, lime, potash, soda, and iron, the non-essential parts of the clay But kaolin is rarely so pure as this, retaining usually more than traces of the potash and soda present in the minerals from which it has been formed, as well as other impurities. The purer it is the less fusible is it and the whiter Now, the china-stone or pe-tun-tse is commonly an altered granite. It is not only of more complex constitution than kaolin, but its variations in composition are greater. It consists, in great proportion, of slightly altered felspar, of a micaceous mineral, and of silica in the form of quartz; it also contains some kaolin. It is fusible at a high temperature owing to the alkalies it contains. Felspar, which is one of the minerals in Cornish stone or pe-tun-tse, is also employed alone or in admixture with other substances, in glazing hard porcelain, and in the preparation of the body or paste of so-called parian china. It should be added that pipe-clay and many other clays are generally impure varieties of kaolin. To the above-named natural substances used in the making of porcelain must be added soapstone or steatite, a silicate of magnesia containing in 100 parts about 62 of silica, 33 of magnesia, and 5 of water. Bone-ash, a most important part of all English soft porcelain, is prepared by burning bones in contact with the air, and contains in 100 parts 83 of phosphate of lime, 12 of carbonate of lime, and 1 of fluoride of calcium. The other constituents of soft porcelain are mostly such as heated together form a kind of glass.

Now, to return to the beginnings of the manufacture of porcelain in Europe. Of course the production of both hard and soft paste was inspired by the desire to reproduce the delightful material which the Chinese had so long made and had adorned so exquisitely. The first approximate success was reached in the Medician or Florentine translucent ware which dates from 1575-1580. In this, three materials were associated, namely, the porcelain clay of Tretto, near Vicenza, a fine sand and a glassy frit. Specimens are extant in several public and private collections. Mr. Drury Fortnum's three pieces show to what perfection of material and potting the inventor had attained; the paste is translucent and white, the glaze bright and smooth without being glittering, the designs are of Persian character in a good under-glaze blue, and the forms, especially of the ewers, eminently satisfactory. At Venice porcelain is said to have been made as early as 1470, and again in 1519, but no specimens of these manufactures have been yet recognised. The same statement must be made concerning the trials at Ferrara in 1567. Later on, in 1720-1740, and in 1765, porcelain, with much glass in its composition, some of it having oxide of tin also, was made at Venice. At Doccia a soft paste porcelain was made in 1735, and at Capo di Monte, near Naples, in 1736. In Spain factories were established at Buen Retiro (1759) and at Alcora (1764). But the soft paste china works of France were earlier in date and more numerous than those of other countries. The dates of their foundation are believed to range from the last quarter of the seventeenth century onwards to the year 1784. The most celebrated of these manufactories was founded at Vincennes in 1741, but did not produce satisfactory porcelain until 1745. In 1753 it was reorganised, and in 1756 transferred to Sèvres. The celebrated *pâte tendre* there made was composed of chalk, marl, and a large quantity of a glassy frit; in 1768 hard paste was produced at Sèvres, and soon afterwards almost completely displaced the soft paste.

Bottger, at Meissen, under the patronage of Augustus II., Elector of Saxony and King of Poland, first realised in Europe the production of true hard porcelain, equal, if not superior, to that of China, so far as the material of the ware was concerned. It was his knowledge of the proper clay, *Schnorrische weisse Erde*, as it was called, which enabled Bottger to secure success. This earth was found near Aue, Schneeberg, Erzegeberge. Bottger is believed to have made hard porcelain first in the year 1709; he died in 1719. The crossed swords, which were adopted as the distinctive mark of the Saxon porcelain in 1712, have been extensively imitated on the ware of other factories, English as well as foreign, so famous did the porcelain of Dresden become. In spite of every precaution the secret of Meissen was betrayed, hard porcelain being in consequence successively made at

Vienna	in 1718	Neudeck	in 1747
Anspach	,, 1718	Berlin	,, 1750
Bayreuth	,, 1720	Baden	,, 1753
Hochst	,, 1740	Ludwigsberg	,, 1758
St. Petersburg	,, 1744	Limbach	,, 1760

This list by no means exhausts the number of German works where hard porcelain was made in great measure in consequence of the initiative of Bottger at Meissen.

The exact circumstances under which kaolin was first discovered and identified in France are still in dispute. Probably the credit of the discovery and its utilisation belongs to the Comte de Brancas-Lauraguais, who, about the year 1758, found the coveted kaolin in the neighbourhood of Alençon. One of his medallions in bas-relief, in the possession of M. Gasnault, is dated October,

1764.   Gérault, in 1764, also seems to have made hard porcelain at Orléans from the kaolin of St. Yrieix-la-Perche, Guettard followed at Bagnolet in 1765.

As we shall point out in a later chapter of this handbook, there is good reason to conclude that Brancas-Lauraguais was familiar with Cornish kaolin before the date (1766) of his English patent. But to William Cookworthy belongs the credit of having first discovered, not the china-clay merely, but also the chinastone of Cornwall, although his patent followed that of Brancas-Lauraguais at an interval of two years. For details the reader is referred to Chapter VI. of the present volume.

It is now time to offer some remarks upon the classification of porcelains and upon the differences between those called hard and those called soft. Yet it must be owned that it is impossible to formulate a perfect definition of porcelain, for the term embraces many species of ceramic wares, and not only what may be termed varieties. At one end of the series of porcelains may be placed the fine stonewares, hard and distinctly translucent in their thinner parts : at the other end will be found the soft, brittle, and absorbent siliceous pastes held together by the coats of glaze with which they are covered. Somewhere between the two extremes will come the glassy porcelains, where a fine solid and opaque substance is suspended, so to speak, in a transparent vitreous medium. If we bring in the microscope to aid us in the discrimination of these differences and resemblances, we shall find that all the hard porcelains, as well as the stonewares which come nearest to them, have a common and distinctive structure which never occurs in the glassy, phosphatic and siliceous pastes, fired at a lower temperature, which simulate them in outward appearance.

That peculiarity of structure consists in the presence of a vast number of small, straight-ended slender rods called *belonites*, and of many minute granules called *spherulites*, both rods and granules having been formed out of the original materials, but not pre-existing in them : they are embedded in a clear or nearly clear paste, the binding material or cement. This observation helps us to a classification, which, if necessarily imperfect from the very mixed and capricious products with which one has to deal, does, at least, recognise the main characteristics of the different types. It must, however, be borne in mind that the several types often overlap in the case of the mixed bodies or pastes of many English soft porcelains. Our scheme starts from the finer stonewares, such as Dwight's semi-porcelain, the old white salt-glazed ware of Staffordshire and the jasper ware of Josiah Wedgwood: it then tabulates the hard or true porcelains, distinguishing the transparent ground mass or binding material as *cement*, and the opaque part as *substance*:—

CLASSIFICATION OF ENGLISH PORCELAINS.

BODY.		GLAZE.	FACTORIES.
Cement.	Substance.		(i. and ii. refer to periods.)
FELSPAR.	Kaolin . . .	Felspar . . Lime . . . Potash, &c. .	Plymouth. Bristol. New Hall.
GLASS . .	Chalk . . .	Red Lead. . White Lead.	Chelsea i. Worcester ii.
	Steatite . .	Nitre. . . . Salt . . . . Potash . . . Soda	Worcester i. Bow ii. Chelsea ii. Worcester ii.
	Bone-ash . .	Smalt . . . Silica . . . Borax . . .	Derby. Caughley.

Of course many other materials were introduced into the "body" besides the chief or characteristic ones named in the table. Of these accessory ingredients the more important were, silica in the form of quartz, flint or white sand, pipe-clay, gypsum, marl, and alum. And then, too, it must be remembered that the glass which formed the artificial cementing material of the soft or artificial porcelains was not always or even generally introduced in the shape of actual glass, but in that of the constituents of glass, which were first "fritted" or heated with some of the constituents of the ware and then admixed with the rest.

One of the most characteristic differences between hard porcelain and soft is the greater porosity of the latter. It is almost impossible to stain any kind of kaolinic or true porcelain body with coloured or greasy substances, so compact has its substance become at the high temperature of the kiln. On the other hand, many of the soft paste porcelains (for example, Bow) are so full of minute cavities, while their ingredients are so imperfectly associated, that discolouration by use has almost invariably occurred. The appearance of fractured surfaces of the two kinds of paste generally differs a good deal. The hard paste presents a nearly smooth, curved surface, with a moderate lustre and slight signs of a granular or crystalline texture. The soft paste, when it is not a mere sub-opaque glass, is of irregular fracture, presenting a dry, rather dull, and non-crystalline surface.

Although the natural or felspathic porcelains are generally hard, and the artificial or vitreous porcelains generally soft, there are variations in this character in both types. Thus many specimens of Worcester porcelain, in which the alkaline constituents have been reduced to a minimum, are almost as hard as the inferior or cottage kaolinic china made at Bristol. A hard body and a hard glaze, it should be added, generally go together, but there is nothing to prevent a soft and fusible glaze (provided the difficulty of unequal contraction in the kiln be got over) from being applied to a china body of a considerable degree of hardness. So, on the other hand, one often finds the soft, porous, nearly opaque body of old Bow porcelain coated with a glaze less easily abraded than the body. One condition to be fulfilled in all such cases is the greater power of resistance to the softening and fusing power of heat which the body must enjoy in comparison with the glaze. It is needful to bear these facts in mind when examining a piece of porcelain said to be of soft paste. Ascertain, by a file, or by a piece of quartz or of felspar, the hardness of the paste on some part of the vessel free from glaze, and do not be content with any signs of attrition which the glaze may show. And it may be further remarked that the removal of the enamel colours by wear is by no means a sign of the porcelain body beneath being of soft paste, but points rather to the hardness of the glaze or to the low temperature at which the enamel-painting on its surface has been burnt in. A good illustration in point is furnished by a cup and saucer of very hard oriental porcelain which is known to have been decorated at Bow. The piece (S.K.M. No. 513'73) shows that the heat of the English enamelling kiln, adapted only to soft paste porcelain covered with a vitreous glaze and to the corresponding enamel colours, has been quite incompetent to effect any proper union between the soft enamels and the hard glaze beneath. The colours have consequently remained dry and rough above the glazed surface, and have suffered greatly in consequence by abrasion.

In mentioning the first manufacture of hard porcelain in England we have referred to the discoveries of Brancas-Lauraguais and Cookworthy. But it should be stated that some early attempts in the same direction were made by Dwight at Fulham and Place at York. But china-clay and china-stone were not known to these two potters, and such specimens of their wares as are now extant are nothing more than fine stoneware, unless, indeed, we accept as English certain white and translucent but roughly-finished jugs and cups which resemble the jugs of Fulham and the cups of York in form, but are now regarded by most ceramic connoisseurs as of Chinese origin. Even if kaolin and pe-tun-tse had been known in this country in the seventeenth century, it must not be forgotten that the distance between china-clay and china-ware is often a very wide one. But a sort of imitative porcelain was regularly made in England just before the middle of the eighteenth century. The early history of three out of four of our oldest and most famous works remains obscure, but we have no evidence to show that any of them were in operation much before the year 1745: it is probable that all—Chelsea, Bow, Derby, and Worcester—were started within a very few years of that date. But, as we have before stated, the china made in all these places was not true porcelain; it was only an ingenious and beautiful counterfeit of the ware it purposed to reproduce. Not inaccurately was it called *artificial* porcelain, being thus distinguished from the oriental material made wholly of natural substances. Not till 1766 or 1768 was the manufacture of this accomplished in England. The former date may be accepted if the Count Brancas-Lauraguais really did make hard porcelain here under his English patent the latter date marks the perfectly authenticated success of Cookworthy in this direction. R. Champion at Bristol, and afterwards a company of potters in Staffordshire, continued to make true porcelain for some years, but the manufacture, unlike that of several continental centres of ceramic industry, never developed into a large and flourishing business Once more the artificial porcelains displaced the natural, and, with some variation in their constituents and their glazes, became (and still remain) the sole product of English china works.

A few words ought now to be said concerning the localities in which English china was made, and the sources of such artistic inspiration as it could claim. With regard to the first point it should be noted that so long as wood was the only fuel used in the kilns, and so long as the productions of the works were intended to be looked upon as mainly decorative or ornamental, any place provided with facilities of water-carriage was adopted for the site of a factory. It was, in fact, mainly by reason of the accident of their residence in Plymouth and Bristol respectively that Cookworthy and Champion established their works in localities not far removed from the quarries of china-clay and china-stone which they employed. The Chelsea factory, it is supposed, originated in some glass works long before carried on in that place. The personal element again comes in with reference to the establishments at Worcester and Derby, where the inventors of the ware happened to live. Not until the more extended use of porcelain for daily requirements had stimulated the competition of cheap manufacture was a single great ceramic centre created. Cheap coal and many varieties of clays, together with numerous facilities for the carriage of the raw materials and finished products, have at last concentrated china-making in the Staffordshire potteries. Bow, Chelsea, Plymouth, and Bristol have long ceased to make porcelain. Derby flickered out in 1848, to be revived within the last few years Worcester has struggled on through many vicissitudes, and with something very much like a break of continuity in 1840, but it has now a great renown for its highly-finished and very varied productions

It is to be feared that a great degree of originality cannot be fairly claimed for English porcelain, even during the best period of its manufacture—1750-1780. Naturally the decorations of the earlier pieces were suggested by, or even directly copied from, Chinese and Japanese enamelled porcelain. The productions of Dresden and Sèvres constituted the chief models of colouring and painting, and even of form, which were continually before the eyes of the managers of the various works in England: even the foreign factory marks were copied or imitated here. Now and then, it is true, a new colour, a fresh style of ornament, a spirited and original set of figures, was produced in England. And it will be found that some of the better-designed groups, vases and cups of Derby, Chelsea, Worcester, and Bristol, are capable of holding their own even in the presence of the beautiful and highly-prized *pâte tendre* of Sèvres. The degradation in form and decoration into which our English china fell after 1780 or 1790 is not without a parallel in the case of the continental factories. We have already spoken of this matter in the Preface to the *Handbook of English Earthenware*, and in that to the present volume, but it is worth while to examine more carefully, in this place, the causes or elements of such degradation.

Besides simply bad ornament, misapplied ornament is too frequently found upon English porcelain of the time to which reference has been made. For instance, decorations of a distinctively eastern type are found associated with forms of vessels as distinctively European in character. Again, designs proper in metal are reproduced in the very different material of porcelain. Once more, we observe vases copied from the severest forms of Greek art painted all over with sprawling sprays of most realistic flowers. Admit that naturalistic flowers are a legitimate decoration for shaped vessels, they certainly seem out of place sometimes, as when we find a full-blown rose, dewdrops and all, in the midst of the gravy on our plate! Even the slight conventionalism of the flowers on Dresden porcelain suffices to prevent flagrant incongruities of this kind.

Landscape tea-services and dessert plates, as painted at Derby and several of the later English china works, further illustrate the use of a kind of decoration, barely legitimate at the best, but thoroughly obnoxious in the form which it generally takes. Such so-called landscapes—"Raglan Castle," the "Menai Bridge"—as duly chronicled on the pieces, originally "feeble sketches of a fiddle-faddle period of art," have lost any pretence of meaning they may once have possessed, through continual copying and re-copying. They have become unreal, without having acquired a legitimate conventionality consonant with their employment for the decoration of table porcelain. How different are they from the refined but broadly-treated landscapes and sea-pieces found upon some of the old Sèvres vases, and, we may add, even from the monochrome landscapes and architectural designs which were occasionally painted upon the porcelain of Worcester and of Bristol!

The decoration of old English porcelain is often bad from the want of power and knowledge in the decorator, often from want of feeling, and often from want of training in the sound principles of ornamentation. From one or other of these defects arises—bad quality of colour and inharmonious arrangements of colours; debasement or misapplication of forms originally good and appropriate; extravagant decoration, especially in the way of overmuch gilding, by which attention is distracted from the more important decorative *motifs* of the pieces; hard and mechanical handling of the brush, and mathematical exactness of form.

But if English porcelain a century ago and onwards to the time of the Great Exhibition of 1851 be generally affected by the serious artistic faults which we have just described, there are happily a great number of pieces of an earlier date which present most commendable features. This will be seen when we study with care the choicer productions of Chelsea, Worcester, and Derby. Even in the darkest time, however, may be traced now and then a happy gleam of fancy, even a flash of original imagination.

CHAPTER II.

CHELSEA.

Origin of the Works—Gouyn and Sprimont—Auction Sales—First Period—Second Period—Chelsea-Derby—Chief Productions—Marks.

THE origin of the porcelain works at Chelsea has not been ascertained: the founder of the factory and the year of its foundation are unknown The earliest dated pieces of Chelsea china are two milk-jugs of the well-known "goat and bee" pattern: these are inscribed beneath, in cursive characters cut in the paste, *Chelsea*, 1745. Clearly they are by no means first attempts, but show that the manufacture had attained at that time a high standard of excellence Then, in the next place, Shaw tells us in his *Rise and Progress of the Staffordshire Potteries* (p. 167), that a number of potters went from Burslem Hot Lane and other places in the potteries to work in the Chelsea china factory in the year 1747. Soon finding, however, "that they were the principal workmen, on whose exertions all the excellence of the porcelain must depend, they resolved to commence business on their own account, at Chelsea, and were in some measure successful." Other early notices of the existence of the Chelsea works are furnished by advertisements in the *London Evening Post* of December 19, 1749, announcing the sale of a freehold messuage in "Great China Row, Chelsea," and in the *General Advertiser* of January 29, 1750, in which mention is made of "Mr. Charles Gouyn, late proprietor and chief manager of the Chelsea House." It is obvious that the factory had been in working order for some time previous to 1750, or the late manager could not then have had, as he announced, large numbers of "curious goods" for disposal A still earlier notice of "Chelsea Porcelaine" must, however, have been inserted in a newspaper of the day, for the advertisement of January 1750 which has been mentioned above was a reply to a previous notice by N. Sprimont, the then manager of the Chelsea factory. This notice by N. Sprimont was repeated on May 15, 1750, if not frequently before that date. The existence of the Chelsea factory somewhere about 1745-1750 is corroborated by the statement in the *London Tradesman*, 1747, of R. Campbell, that "we have lately made some attempts to make porcelain or chinaware after the manner it is done in China and Dresden; there is a house at Greenwich and another at Chelsea, where the undertakers have been for some time trying to imitate that beautiful manufacture."

Thus far we have been introduced to two successive managers of the Chelsea works, Charles Gouyn and Nicolas Sprimont: both we think were of Flemish, not French, nationality. Sprimont, the name of a small town in Flanders, belongs also to an old family of the Duchy of Limbourg, a district where some of the finest stonewares of the sixteenth century were made A fragment of a stoneware jug bearing the Sprimont arms was recently discovered at Bouffioulx near Liége; in the latter town some members of the Sprimont family settled as early as 1600. It is not therefore unreasonable, on the whole, to conclude that Nicolas Sprimont, who succeeded Gouyn in the proprietorship of the Chelsea factory, may have been of Flemish rather than of French origin. Gouyn is itself also a Flemish patronymic.

Perhaps we shall not be deemed too hazardous in conjecture if we note here what may be taken as a confirmation of Sprimont's Flemish origin. An advertisement of January 2, 1764, informs the public that "Mr. Sprimont is advised to go to the German

Spaw." The only continental watering-place then in vogue was Spa in Belgium, a town which is distant from Liége only seventeen miles What more natural than that Nicolas Sprimont, a native of Liége, should seek a renewal of his health by returning to the neighbourhood of his old home?

It should be stated here that N. Sprimont was originally a silversmith of Compton Street, Soho. He entered his name at Goldsmith's Hall, as a plateworker, in January 1742. There is a pair of oval silver-gilt dishes, made by him in 1743, in the Windsor Castle Collection. They have escalloped edges ornamented with shells and corals in high relief. Ornament of this character is frequently found upon Chelsea porcelain.

Although no view or plan of the works is known to be extant, it has been ascertained that the Chelsea factory was situated at the river-end and western side of Lawrence Street. It had a small frontage to the Thames at the end of what is now called Cheyne Walk. That a part of the works was situated in the neighbourhood of Cheyne Row West was proved in 1843 during excavations previous to building some new houses there; large quantities of broken vases and figures were then found. There is extant a portion of a tea-service on which is painted a landscape, including a church, and, adjoining a building like a factory, a round tower, which might be meant for a kiln. As the porcelain, though unmarked, is thought to belong to the early Chelsea time, and as a piece of water, which might be intended for the Thames, is seen in the middle distance, it has been contended that we have here a view of the Chelsea china works. It may be so, but it teaches us nothing, since the features of the scene which remain to the present day are entirely unlike their presentments, and we cannot feel sure that the factory is more exactly figured.

However, the examination of the Chelsea auction catalogues and of the early advertisements of sales, enables us to trace the later stages in the history of these works, and to form some conception of the magnificent specimens which they produced. Of course much ordinary or slightly decorated ware, and many small and unimportant pieces were turned out—in fact, no factory could otherwise, without extraneous subsidies, have been kept going. But still very great credit must be given to Sprimont for the spirit and skill with which he carried on the factory. Had a readier sale and remunerative prices been obtainable for the more sumptuous products of the works, its financial success would have been assured. The exquisitely soft appearance of the body of the early Chelsea porcelain was revealed to advantage in the simpler style and sparse decoration which prevailed in the first period. The rich gilding with the turquoise and crimson grounds which belong to the latter stage of the works—1759-1769—and also the mazarine blue and pea-green colours introduced somewhat earlier, show to what a high degree of technical perfection the Chelsea works had attained before the close of their independent existence and their cession to W. Duesbury of Derby.

An approximate date is given to the period of manufacture of the exquisite scent-bottles by advertisements of sales in 1754 and 1756, and by the year 1759 marked on one of Mr. Franks's beautiful specimens. These bottles frequently bear French inscriptions (sometimes incorrectly spelt), and were long mistaken for productions of the Sèvres manufactory. In one way or another connections may indeed be detected between the foreign and the English works. Take, as an instance, the successive use or discovery at Sèvres and at Chelsea of the superb coloured grounds for which both factories became famous. The claret colour which distinguished Chelsea must have been invented in the year 1759, as examples of it were first included in the sale which took place from April 28th to May 2nd, 1760. This colour was imitated at Sèvres and at Dresden: Chelsea dessert services occur with some pieces made to match at a foreign porcelain works. On the other hand, Sèvres retained an undisputed superiority for its rose-colour, the beautiful "Rose Dubarry." This enamel is seen on some of the finest productions in *pâte tendre*. It was invented by an artist employed in the factory, one Xhrouet, as early as 1757. The choicest specimens of this colour were made between the years 1757 and 1762: as pointed out by the late Baron C. Davillier, it ought to be called "Rose Pompadour." Mazarine blue was probably invented at Chelsea in 1755 or 1756, turquoise-blue and pea-green in 1758 or 1759: a Pompadour colour is named in a Chelsea catalogue dated 1771.

In speaking further of the dates of Chelsea productions and the development of the factory, it may be remarked that a trivial accessory often constitutes an important element in the determination of the period. For example, in a figure or statuette, marks, modelling, enamelling, and finish are not always a sufficient guide to the discovery of the relative dates of similar pieces, but a small incident may betray the period. An illustration in point is furnished by a couple of figures of Falstaff in Mr. R. W. Read's collection. The earlier piece is of Chelsea make, the later of Derby (about 1775), but both are from the same mould. Falstaff's inn-reckoning is given on a small tablet in these different ways:—

Chelsea.			*Derby.*		
Sack	4	0	Capon	3	6
Capon	2	2	Port	5	0
Sauce		4	Bread	2	0
Bread		0½			

The older and more intelligent form of the account is clearly that on the Chelsea figure: one is led to conclude that the term "sack" had become obsolete in the interval. Mr. Willett has a Chelsea figure of Falstaff in which the reckoning runs:—

Capon	2	2
Sauce		4
Sack, 2 galls.	5	6
Anch. and Sack	2	6
Bread		0½
	10	6½

In the Schreiber collection is another example.—

A capon	. . . . . .	2	0
Sauce	. . . . .	4	0
Sack	. . . .	5	0
		11	0

Another useful criterion of age is sometimes furnished by peculiarities of costume, although the use of old moulds interferes more with this test than with that afforded by the special province of the enamel-painter. Thus in a Chelsea figure of Harlequin (marked with the red anchor), he still wears the coat, not the jacket, which bespeaks a later time, and which then occurs on Derby porcelain.

A careful study of the sale catalogues of Chelsea china serves to show the important developments occurring in the works. In 1754, when the quantity of porcelain made had become very considerable, the first sale by auction took place. It occupied fifteen days. The following is a list of subsequent sales so far as Mr. Nightingale's inquiries have informed us:—

1754. December 16th to 20th. } "Enamelled on white."
1755. March 10th to 27th.

1756. March and April, sixteen days. Mazarine blue introduced.
1759. March and April. Pea-green colour introduced.
1760. April 28th to May 2nd. Claret colour and turquoise.
1761. April 30th to May 5th.
1763. March, eleven days.
1769. May.
1770. February, four days.

It is probable that no porcelain was made at Chelsea by Sprimont after 1768. In 1770, on February 5th, the transfer of the works, models in wax, brass, lead, &c., to W. Duesbury of Derby, was completed. Sales by auction of the produce of the

Chelsea works under their new management were held in 1772, 1773, 1777, and then in each year until 1785

Sometimes these old catalogues enable one to trace the history of individual pieces of Chelsea porcelain. For instance, one of the lots sold on the 10th February. 1773, by Mr. Christie, consisted of:

"A pair of caudle-cups and covers and stands finely enamelled in compartments, with antique jars and crimson and gold curtains, 2*l* 3*s*. *Lord Apsley*."

Now, in the Alexandra Palace, No 1304 was a part of the above lot, lent for exhibition by the late Lord Bathurst, the descendant of Lord Apsley, and described thus —

"Two-handled chocolate cup, cover, and stand, pink festoons and green urns in medallions, Chelsea, gold anchor mark."

In reality the festoons were curtains or drapery of crimson and gold. Happily the companion cup still remains in the present Earl Bathurst's possession. At Wardour Castle are still preserved three fine pieces of Chelsea porcelain purchased at Christie's on the 17th February, 1770, by the then Lord Arundel, who gave 4*l*. 7*s*. for "a most beautiful caudle-cup, cover, and saucer, of the rich mazarine blue and gold, inimitably enamell'd in pastoral figures"; and 13*l*. for "Two satyr bottles of the mazarine blue, embellish'd with burnish'd gold grapes, highly finish'd with gold birds, most curiously chas'd."

So far as the body or paste of the porcelain is concerned the productions of the Chelsea factory may be grouped in two divisions. The first of these probably extended in date from the commencement of the works until the year 1757; the second includes the years 1759 to 1769. During the first period the porcelain was generally characterised by considerable translucency, much glassy frit being employed in the paste, and the glaze being also very soft. The factory must then have been in most active operation, for a single year's production (excluding the pieces sold by private sale) took sixteen days to dispose of by public auction. The catalogue of

FIG. 1.—CHELSEA: SCENT BOTTLE. SCHREIBER COLLECTION.

FIG. 2.—CHELSEA: SNUFF BOX. SCHREIBER COLLECTION.

FIG. 3.—CHELSEA: SNUFF BOX. SCHREIBER COLLECTION.

FIG. 4.—CHELSEA: CHINESE FIGURE; EARLY PERIOD.

that auction (in 1756) comprised over 1,600 lots, and more than 6,500 pieces. In 1757 the activity of the works slackened, ceasing in 1758, the manfacture being resumed in 1759. From that date all the china made at Chelsea was, we believe, phosphatic, that is, it contained bone-ash in the body; also the use of gold in its decoration became at that time more frequent and more lavish; figures with gilding upon them are not indeed so much as mentioned in the sale catalogue of 1756. There is a frequent peculiarity of the earlier body which may be named here. It was first noticed by Dr. H. W. Diamond that the soft waxen pieces of Chelsea porcelain, which belong to the first period, often exhibit, when we view a candle through them, a number of moon-like discs, scattered about the pieces irregularly, and more translucent than the rest of the material. They seem to be due to an irregular and excessive aggregation of that vitreous part of the frit which formed so large a constituent of the early body. Sprimont, on succeeding to the ownership and management of the works about the year 1749, introduced several changes into them, extending not merely to the forms and decoration of the pieces, but to the substance of the ware itself. The use of bone-ash at Bow, since 1748, had probably become quickly known to the Chelsea manager, who forthwith followed this practice. Anyhow, bones are found, by chemical analysis of specimens of Chelsea china which obviously belong to the second period of the fabrique, but long before its acquisition by Duesbury, to form about 45 per cent. of their constituents. An analysis of a Chelsea figure marked with the gold anchor, but decorated in the colours and style of the early Sprimont period, gave in 100 parts:—

Silica . . . . . . 40·2	Phosphoric acid . . 20·3
Alumina . . . . 8·4	Magnesia . . . trace
Iron oxide . . . 1·2	Soda . . . 1·0
Lime . . . . . 27·4	Potash . . . . ·9

These numbers resemble those found in the analysis of Bow

porcelain, although the alumina in the latter is higher, and the phosphoric acid and lime of the former somewhat lower [1] (see page 29). It is not indeed to be assumed that the original unctuous-looking frit body of the earlier time was wholly abandoned by Sprimont at once ; probably it and the bone-body were made contemporaneously until the latter soon wholly superseded the former. Of the extant specimens of Chelsea porcelain it may safely be said that over 90 per cent. are of the bone-body.

Mr Nightingale's researches into the early history of the Chelsea factory have led to the discovery of a number of advertisements and auction catalogues, from which much information may be gleaned as to the styles prevalent at different times. For example, in 1756 the pieces were nearly all decorated in enamel on a white ground with little or no gilding, the decoration mainly consisting of "flowers, buds, insects, and Indian plants." The models included vases, beakers, figures, scent-bottles, groups, dessert services, lustres, branched candlesticks, and girandoles In 1759 vases and other pieces in rich ground colours, with much gilding, first appear. The sauce-boats, large tureens in the form of boars' heads, swans, &c. ; the vessels and dishes in the shape of leaves, flowers, and vegetables, and the crawfish salts, are, however, all of early date. Our figures (1, 2, 3) represent three of the early scent-bottles and boxes now in the Schreiber collection. Fig. 4 is an early figure in the oriental style in a private collection ; Fig. 5 is a leaf-shaped dish from the Jermyn Street collection. When these pieces are marked they bear the anchor enamelled in red, purple, or brown, or the anchor in relief on a raised oval Sprimont's peculiarly extravagant and rococo taste is seen in the form of the vase, 827 '82 (Fig. 6). The great British Museum vase is in the same style ; its date is 1765

[1] Another figure of Chelsea porcelain, also marked with the gold anchor, but belonging to the Duesbury period (1770-1784), contained 40·3 per cent. of silica, but only 13 9 of phosphoric acid.

FIG. 5.—CHELSEA: DESSERT DISH.   MUSEUM OF PRACTICAL GEOLOGY.

FIG. 6.—CHELSEA: VASE, ROCOCO STYLE. JONES BEQUEST. SOUTH KENSINGTON MUSEUM. NO. 827, '82.

FIG. 7.—CHELSEA: THE FIFER. SCHREIBER COLLECTION.

CHELSEA.

The period 1759-1769 is represented by a pair of figures of the "fifer" and "drummer" (Figs. 7 and 8) in the Schreiber collection, and by the richly adorned heart-shaped vase in the Jones Bequest (Fig. 9); this piece bears the anchor mark in gold.

The Derby-Chelsea period, 1770-1784, is illustrated by the "Coopers'" bowl (Fig. 10), which is the Schreiber gift, and which reveals some symptoms of the influence exerted on Chelsea by the Derby artists; this bowl is in the Schreiber gift. The vase No. 825 '82, though marked with the gold anchor only, is of Derby-Chelsea character. The winged demi-figures serving as handles are of white biscuit (see Fig. 11). The covered bowl, Fig. 12, probably belongs here.

Besides the indications afforded in the preceding part of the present chapter, as to the extent, character, and variety of the productions of Chelsea, something ought be said concerning the more famous of its statuettes. In the sale catalogue of 1756 more than forty varieties of figures and groups were included. Amongst these are found—monkeys playing on musical instruments; the Madonna and Child, standing on a globe and holding a cross; a map seller; a cobbler and wife singing; a group of Europe and Asia, and one of Africa and America, Perseus and Andromeda; a set of five figures emblematic of the senses. These early statuettes were either without any gilding or were very sparingly adorned with gold. After 1759 the more gorgeously coloured and the richly gilt figures were extensively produced. Amongst these may be named many of the copies of the well known four quarters of the globe; the "antique seasons;" the Welsh tailor and his wife on goats; Shakespeare, Milton, and Sir Isaac Newton; Apollo and the nine Muses; George III. in a Vandyke dress leaning on an altar; Una and the lion, twenty-seven inches high, and Britannia of the same height; a copy of this last piece sold, in 1875, for 157*l*. 10*s*. Scores of other figures and groups might be named here—actors and actresses, politicians, distinguished military and naval commanders, royal personages (mostly modelled from contemporary paintings and engravings), and subjects from Greek and Roman history or mythology. The 'Music Lesson,' Fig. 13, and the statuette of 'Lord Chatham' (Fig. 14) are good examples of these fine groups. Copies or adaptations from the figures made at foreign factories were often produced at Chelsea; of these the "Nourrice" of Palissy is a good example. Merely to catalogue such productions would demand a larger space than that allotted to the whole subject of Chelsea factory in this small handbook. Much information as to these figures and groups may be gleaned from Mr Nightingale's *Contributions*. From that work we must content ourselves with quoting a single example of such pieces in order to show the difference of prices between 1773 and 1874. "A large group of Jason and Medea, vowing before the altar of Diana, enamelled and richly finished with gold" brought three guineas at Christie's in Pall Mall in the former year, but was sold for 29*l*. 10*s*. in 1883 in the King Street rooms.

Allusion has been made before (p. 22) to various vessels of Chelsea porcelain in the form of plants and animals. Many of these belong to the first period—1745-1756—of the factory. In the auction sale of 1756 occur numerous examples, melons, pineapples, apples, lemons, oranges, figs, cauliflowers, bunches of flowers, and grapes; also of cabbages, artichokes, and sunflowers. Amongst animals we find tureens, sauce-boats, and dishes representing boars' heads, swans, ducks, partridges, cocks and hens, cows, sheep, goats, dogs, and foxes. To the same early period belong the lightly ornamented square and hexagonal cups and saucers and the white dessert dishes in the form of leaves, having chocolate-coloured edges and reddish veinings, with sprays of enamelled flowers, for their ornamentation.

An anchor in relief in a raised oval cartouche is the earliest regular Chelsea mark, although the name Chelsea, with an incised triangle, has been found on two or three pieces (see p. 14). The

FIG. 9.—CHELSEA: VASE. JONES BEQUEST. SOUTH KENSINGTON MUSEUM.
No. 828, '82.

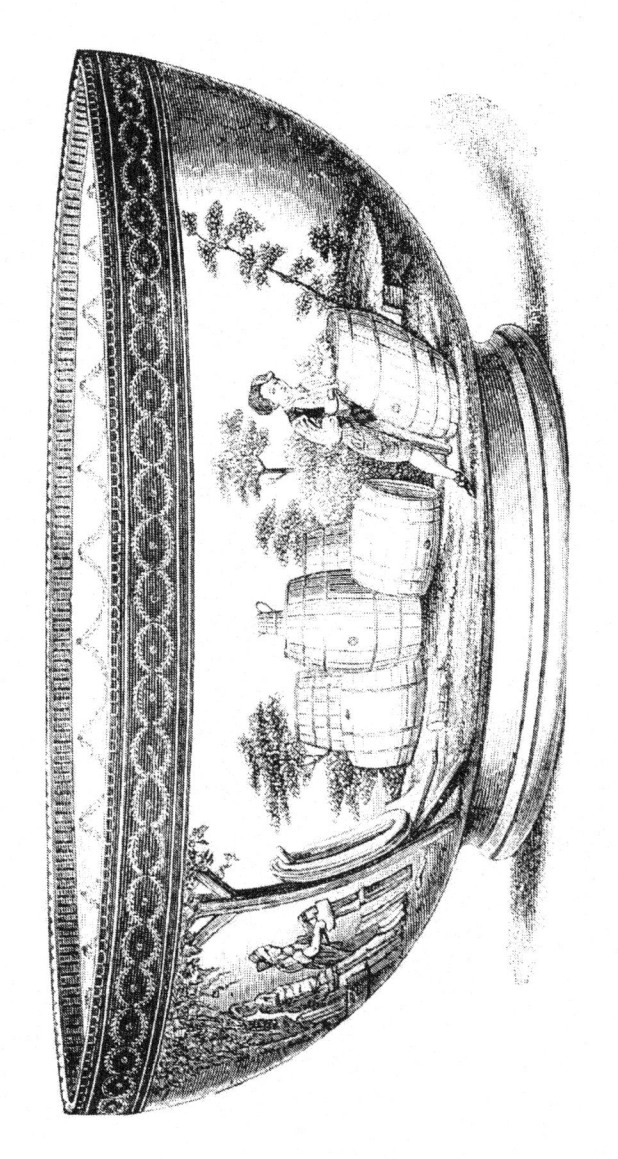

FIG. 10.—CHELSEA—DERBY: THE COOPERS' BOWL. SCHREIBER COLLECTION.

FIG. 11.—CHELSEA—DERBY: VASE WITH BISCUIT HANDLES. JONES BEQUEST. SOUTH KENSINGTON MUSEUM. NO. 825, '82.

FIG. 12.—CHELSEA—DERBY: COMPOTIER, STAND AND COVER.
SCHREIBER COLLECTION.

FIG. 13—CHELSEA: THE MUSIC LESSON, AFTER ROUBILIAC. SCHREIBER COLLECTION.

FIG. 14.—CHELSEA: EARL OF CHATHAM. SCHREIBER COLLECTION.

attempt to assign the raised anchor to the Bow factory is not a happy one. The pieces of porcelain on which it occurs are of an early and simple type without gilding, and are of the rich unctuous-looking paste previously described as characteristic of early Chelsea. Their technique is higher than that of the early Bow pieces, and they are not phosphatic, that is, they contain no bone-ash. Sometimes the raised anchor is relieved in colour (on a white ground) with a brownish-red enamel, as on a pair of small birds belonging to Dr. Diamond.

The anchor in red, purple, or gold is the more usual Chelsea mark, and was continued to the close of the works. The coloured mark is generally earlier than that in gold, the latter being naturally used for pieces which were enriched with gilding. The anchor is sometimes very roughly pencilled, while its size varies a good deal, though it is never so large as the anchor mark found on Venetian porcelain. Why this mark was appropriated by the Chelsea factory we cannot tell, but it is not improbable that it was adopted from that of Venice. In this connection it is interesting to recall the fact that a manufactory of glass was founded at Chelsea in 1676 by some Venetians, under the auspices of the Duke of Buckingham.

We would call attention, before closing this brief story of the Chelsea factory, to the example of successful potting and firing furnished by the large dish in the South Kensington Museum, No. 172 '65. It is nearly 17 inches across. The decoration consists of beautifully painted animals and bouquets of flowers.

CHAPTER III.

BOW.

Early history—Introduction of bone-ash into china—Characteristic productions—Marks.

It is not known at what time the china factory at Bow or Stratford-le-Bow was founded. Probably it originated with the patent, dated December 6th, 1744, taken out by Heylyn and Frye Edward Heylyn, of Bow, is described as a merchant, Thomas Frye, of West Ham, Essex, as a painter. Their patent was for the production of a porcelain, containing, amongst other ingredients, "an earth, the produce of the Cherokee nation in America, called by the natives *unaker*" Frye became manager of the works, probably from their commencement; he remained in that position until his resignation from ill-health in 1759: he died in 1762. The first owners of the Bow factory, so far as is known, were two merchants,—Weatherby and John Crowther, whose partnership dates from 1750. Weatherby died in 1762: Crowther became bankrupt in 1763, although he seems to have retained an interest in the Bow works for some years afterwards This continued connection of Crowther with the Bow factory is corroborated by the inscriptions on two Bow plates in the Willett collection. Both bear in the centre the initials in blue, R.C.; one however is also inscribed on the back thus:

Mr. Robert Crowther
Stockport
Cheshire
1770.

Probably this Robert Crowther was a brother or near relative of the Bow proprietor. Advertisements relating to Bow china occur in *Aris's Birmingham Gazette* during 1753. One of these, on March 5th, relates to the opening of a Bow china warehouse in Cornhill; another is addressed to "all painters in the Blue and White Potting Way, and Enamellers on China-Ware," and to "Painters brought up in the Snuff-Box Way, Japanning, Fan-painting, &c.:" it further states that "at the same House, a Person is wanted who can model small Figures in Clay neatly." In the *Public Advertiser*, of March, 1757, a sale by auction of services and curious and ornamental pieces, the production of the Bow Porcelain Manufactory, is advertised. The next year there were two sales, in which were included figure groups, jars, beakers, birds and beasts, and tea and other table services, while the pieces were of enamelled china as well as of plain blue and white. In 1764 the stock of John Crowther was sold.

The Bow works were called New Canton, as we learn from the Bow memorandum books in Lady C. Schreiber's collection, as well as from some inkstands made at Bow and inscribed "Made at New Canton," the dates 1750 and 1751 being also on these pieces. This fact is in accordance with the statement of Thomas Craft, a Bow painter, to whom we shall presently refer, that the Bow factory was copied from that at Canton in China. In the year 1776 the Bow works were purchased by W. Duesbury, of Derby, and the moulds and models sent there.

Very important information concerning the Bow works was derived from some excavations made on the site by Messrs. Bell and Black, in the year 1868. While trenching a drain from the lucifer-match works to the sewer, the workmen found, at a depth of eight or ten feet below the surface, a number of fragments of glazed and unglazed porcelain, both white and painted in blue, as well as fragments of saggers and wasters. Not the least interesting of these finds was a circular cake of frit, now in the Jermyn Street Museum (H 19), where also are preserved many other specimens found at the same time, including broken shell dessert-stands, and pieces of white porcelain with the *prunus*, or so-called may-flower, in relief upon them. The importance of this discovery close to the site of one of the Bow kilns is considerable, as by its means it has been possible to assign with certainty to Bow many pieces of soft porcelain previously attributed wrongly to other factories.

Before the discovery of these Bow relics and of the memorandum books of the works previously named, our knowledge of the Bow factory was most meagre, and indeed in great part inexact. The most prominent documentary evidence relating to it was afforded by a manuscript memorandum in the lid of a case in the British Museum. This case inclosed a punch-bowl of Bow porcelain painted by Thomas Craft, in 1760. The document was written in 1790, and described the bowl as painted in "the old Japan taste, a taste at the time much esteemed by the then Duke of Argyle." We learn moreover that the piece was burnt at Mr. Gyles's kiln at Kentish Town—the same Gyles who advertised somewhat misleadingly, with reference to Worcester china, in 1768, "that the enamelling Branch is performed in London by the said J. Giles." Craft tells us that the Bow works afforded employment to 300 persons, including about ninety painters and about 200 turners, throwers, &c —all under one roof.

Before describing some important and characteristic pieces of Bow porcelain, and before endeavouring to point out the characters by which the body glaze and painting may be distinguished from those of other fabriques, it will be useful to return to the subject of the Bow patents.

The two patents taken out in connection with the Bow works disclose two essentially different porcelain-bodies. The 1744 specification of Edward Heylyn and Thomas Frye gives, as the ingredients, one part of potash, one part of sand or flint, and from one to four parts of a kind of porcelain-clay called *unaker*, from which the sand and mica had been removed by washing, from the Cherokee territory, North America: the glaze contained seven of potash-glass to one of *unaker*. In the second patent, taken out by T. Frye, November 17th, 1748, the *unaker* is replaced by other materials. Two parts of a virgin-earth, produced by the calcination of certain animals, vegetables and fossils, are directed to be mixed with one part of flint or sand and fritted; then of this frit two parts are taken and mixed with one part of pipe-clay. The glaze was made of red lead, saltpetre and sand, with some white lead and smalts. There can be no difficulty in identifying the earth produced by the calcination of certain animal and vegetable matters with bone-earth, that is, calcined bones which consist mainly of phosphate of lime. The patentee, of course, did not desire to be too explicit. Here are some analytical results confirming this deduction. They were obtained by means of a careful chemical examination of some fragments of glazed and unglazed porcelain, disinterred during the draining operations at the works of Messrs. Bell and Black, at Bow, previously mentioned.—

	Per Cent.		*Per Cent.*
Silica	40·0	Phosphoric acid	17·3
Alumina	16·0	Magnesia	·8
Iron Oxide	*trace*	Soda	1·3
Lime	24·0	Potash	·6

An easy calculation suffices to show that the proportion of bone-ash which was used to make this porcelain-body must have corresponded very closely with the amount (44 3 per cent.) which T. Frye directed to be employed. Now as the fragments of porcelain which gave the above results were clearly *wasters*, there can be no doubt that they represent productions of the Bow factory. Moreover, being of early date (though the lead glaze proved they were not made under the 1744 patent), they serve to confirm the conclusion, drawn from the wording of the 1748 patent, that bone was first used at Bow as an ingredient of porcelain. Analyses of porcelains made at Chelsea, Worcester, Liverpool and Caughley during the second half of the eighteenth century prove, however, that the employment of bone-ash was very widely extended about the year 1760. This is clear from the following paragraph which we cite from *The Handmaid of the Arts* (1758), vol. ii. p 342:—

"The following composition will produce wares which will have the properties of the true china, if they be rightly managed in the manufacture. Take of the best white sand, or calcined flints finely powdered, 20 lbs, add to it of very white pearlashes 5 lbs., of bones calcined to perfect whiteness, 2 lbs"

So the frequent attribution to Josiah Spode the younger (about the years 1797–1800) of the first introduction of bone-ash into the paste of English porcelain must be regarded as destitute of any basis of fact. To assume that he at least fixed the best proportion of bone-ash to be employed is negatived by the evidence afforded by the chemical analysis of specimens of English soft porcelain made at many famous factories long before Spode's time. If there be one ingredient in these porcelains of which constancy in amount can be predicated more than any other, it is either the silica or the phosphate of lime, but, in most cases, the latter.

In endeavouring to separate the productions of Bow from those of Chelsea and of other factories there are very great difficulties. The pieces were more frequently unmarked than marked, even if we are right in assigning such signs as the dagger or Latin cross associated with an anchor, and an arrow with an annulet on the shaft, to the Essex factory. The only sure guides which connoisseurs possess at present are founded on a comparison of the paste and decoration of Craft's bowl in the British Museum, and of the fragments disinterred on the site of the Bow works, with such extant specimens of old soft porcelain which might otherwise be attributed to Chelsea The Bow memorandum books and advertisements of sales before referred to, aid us in making such

FIG. 15.—BOW: SOUP TUREEN, WHITE. SOUTH KENSINGTON MUSEUM. No. 307, '69.

FIG. 16.—BOW: DESSERT DISH. MUSEUM OF PRACTICAL GEOLOGY.

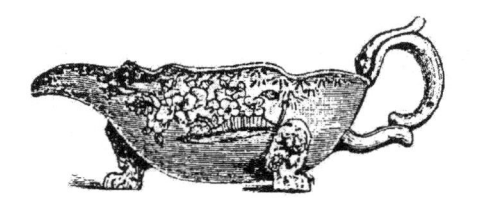

FIG. 17.—BOW: SAUCE BOAT, WITH BLUE PAINTING. MUSEUM OF PRACTICAL GEOLOGY.

FIG. 18.—BOW: PLATE WITH BIRDS AND FESTOONS. SCHREIBER COLLECTION.

comparisons, but cannot alone be relied on, since the forms and styles of decoration named in these documents were common to Chelsea and to Bow. In our illustrations of the productions of the Bow works we will begin with specimens which are of undoubted Bow make. The first of these (Fig. 15) is a white tureen decorated with the may-flower or prunus pattern in high relief. It is in the South Kensington Museum (No. 307 '69), and is a perfectly characteristic example. The ware is generally of great thickness, but remarkably translucent in its thinner parts, where the transmitted light appears somewhat yellowish, not greenish, as in Worcester. The glaze is nearly white, but verges sometimes upon a faint straw colour; it has collected in considerable quantity about the reliefs. It contains much lead, and is liable to become iridescent and discoloured.

The next figure (Fig. 16) represents a dessert dish in the form of a scallop shell. It has a narrow border of red and gold; the centre is delicately painted with the so-called "partridge pattern" or quail and wheatsheaf pattern, of which frequent mention is made in the MS. notes of John Bowcocke, of Bow. The same pattern is found on Worcester, Chelsea, and Bristol porcelain: the present piece, which is H 26 in the Jermyn Street collection, almost certainly belongs to Bow.

A third example of Bow is furnished by the sauce-boat, with under-glaze blue painted border, shown in Fig. 17. This piece (H 54 in the Jermyn Street collection), is identical in form and in the colour of the blue used with sauce-boats of which fragments have been found on the site of the works.

In the Schreiber collection are many statuettes, plates, vases, and other pieces variously and richly ornamented, which have been attributed to Bow by the late Mr. Schreiber and Lady Charlotte Schreiber. These attributions have been founded upon such intimate knowledge of all the evidence available for the identification of this manufacture of porcelain that they may be accepted with a large measure of confidence. Further researches and new evidence may shake some of these conclusions, but, there is good reason to suppose that the large majority of the pieces called Bow in the Schreiber Gift are really authentic specimens of that factory. A plate (Fig. 18) is one of these pieces. It is delicately decorated, after a mixed oriental style, with fighting cocks and a festooned floral border, in rich enamel colours and gilding A group, fifteen inches high, of Britannia with a medallion of George II (Fig 19), and a hexagonal vase with applied floral wreaths in high relief and a mask on either side (Fig 20), are likewise considered to have been made at the Bow works, and may be taken as representative pieces of their respective kinds.

It should be stated that transfer printing both under and over the glaze was adopted at an early period in the Bow works. In Fig. 19 the outlines of the ornaments on the dress and stand are transfer printed.

Amongst other figures often attributed to Bow the following subjects have been found, the specimens in some cases being marked with the anchor and dagger in red :—Harlequin, Columbine and Pierrot, H. Woodward[1] as a " fine gentleman;" and Kitty Clive[1] as Mrs. Riot, in Garrick's farce of *Lethe;* Peg Woffington, Chatterton, and a waterman with Doggett's badge Of symbolic, domestic, and rustic statuettes may be named—a set of four seated figures representing the seasons, Fame ; a seated Venus and Cupid; the cooks, a man carrying a dish of fowls, and a woman with a dish of ham ; a pair of figures of a boy and girl dancing, each in a bosquet of foliage and flowers. Many of these last-named statuettes have nozzles for candles. It has been stated, apparently with reason, that a square hole at the back of such pieces is found only in the figures emanating from the Bow works, and not in those made at Chelsea.

Amongst characteristic pieces of Bow porcelain in the Jermyn Street collection we would name two fine vases (H 28 and 29),

---

[1] These figures were certainly made at Chelsea.

Fig. 19.—BOW: BRITANNIA WITH MEDALLION OF GEORGE II. SCHREIBER COLLECTION.

FIG. 20.—BOW: VASE WITH WREATHS AND MASKS.   SCHREIBER COLLECTION.

like our Fig. 20; five examples of the embossed may-flower pattern (H 1 to H 4 *a*); two sauce-boats (H 53, 54); eleven white embossed knife-handles (H 5 to H 17), an inkstand (H 23), several pieces of the partridge or quail pattern, and a number of figures and other pieces marked with an anchor and dagger in red enamel (H 45 to 48) One of these has an italic capital *B* in under-glaze blue. There are very many pieces of porcelain attributed to Bow in the Schreiber collection.

Of the marks supposed to belong to Bow the commonest is the anchor and dagger in red enamel—The italic *B* is rarely found, but the arrow with an annulet on the shaft is not very uncommon; however, it occurs, it must be owned, on pieces of porcelain (Jermyn Street collection, H 52), which are of harder paste and colder in hue than the usual Bow porcelain. A small crescent in blue has also been regarded as a Bow mark. The shell sweetmeat-stands so frequently occurring in collections of English china are rarely marked; some of hard paste belong to Plymouth and Bristol, others to Worcester, and others (such as H 30 and H 31 in the Jermyn Street collection) without doubt to Bow. Some vases which have been very reasonably assigned to Bow on the score of the quality of their paste, and the general style and peculiar colour of their (under glaze) blue decoration, are marked, under the glaze, in blue, with a monogram of T and F conjoined. Thomas Frye signed his own engravings sometimes with this monogram, although in his own portrait, mezzo-tinted in 1760, italic capitals occur. There can be no doubt that pieces of Bow china bearing this monogram were painted by Thomas Frye himself. They must be attributed to an early period of the Bow works— before 1760. Frye's published works prove him to have been an accomplished artist; he was a painter and miniaturist as well as an engraver.

The well-known "goat and bee" milk-jugs, of which there are

two specimens from Strawberry Hill (one white, one coloured) in Jermyn Street, were once attributed to Bow. They bear an incised triangle of considerable size, cut in the paste before firing. Three other pieces in the same collection, namely, a tea-pot, a *sucrier*, and a small figure of an infant (II 35, 36, 37), bear the same mark. As, however, two other "goat and bee" jugs—having the same triangle, accompanied by the word Chelsea, also incised and the date 1745—are known, it must be regarded as almost certain that none of these pieces were made at Bow. Quite recently a pair of these goat-jugs in silver, with the date-letter of 1739, have been acquired by Mr. H. Willett.

CHAPTER IV.

DERBY

Origin obscure—Duesbury—Bloor—Marks—Crown-Derby—Biscuit Figures.

THE exact origin of one only of the five great English porcelain works started in the eighteenth century, that of Worcester, has been ascertained. Of the founding of the Derby factory very little is known : we believe that the tradition is entirely without corroboration which speaks of "small china figures of animals and other ornaments, manufactured by a foreigner in Lodge Lane about the year 1745." Ten years later, when W Duesbury of Longton is described as an "enameller," a certain Andrew Planché of Derby is called a "chinamaker." This is perplexing, for Duesbury, according to some writers, had already built, in 1751, the famous Derby factory in the Nottingham Road. He was, however, then living in London, where he remained until 1755 or 1756. A. Planché, too, cannot have been the "foreigner" who started porcelain figure-making in Derby in 1745, for he was but seventeen at that time. We are told by Mr. Ll. Jewitt that Duesbury had no connection with the Derby factory until 1756. Yet its productions had attained great excellence by that time, as Mr. Nightingale has shown in his *Contributions*, p. lxvii. For in December, 1756, there was an auction sale in London, lasting four days, by order of the "Proprietors of the Derby Porcelain Manufactory," of "a curious collection of fine figures, jars, sauce-boats, services for desserts . . after the finest Dresden models." Again, in 1757, there appeared a paragraph in the *Public Advertiser* in which it was stated that many good judges could not distinguish the Derby figures from those made at Dresden. It is incredible that any productions, at all deserving such praise, could have been made at a factory which had not been in existence for more than eighteen months. But if we are in doubt about the proprietors and managers of the Derby works prior to 1756, we are equally in doubt as to the exact nature of the Derby productions of that early period. Mr Nightingale suggests that some of the unmarked figures hitherto attributed to the Bow factory may really be of early Derby make. It is probable that this is the case, and that a very careful comparison of a large number of such figure pieces would result in their being distributed between the three factories of Bow, Derby, and Longton Hall. Besides the unmarked pieces there are some pieces having dubious marks not yet assigned with certainty to any one factory, although some of them have been spoken of as mere workmen's signs. One or more of these marks may really belong to the early Derby time.

In or about the year 1758 the Derby works were enlarged, and the number of hands employed doubled; the abandonment of the Longton Hall factory at this time may be connected with such an augmentation of the Derby establishment. Our information with regard to these works and their productions is most meagre between the years 1758 and 1770, being almost entirely confined to a few items in sales by auction of Derby figures, candlesticks, baskets, and jars. But in 1769 W Duesbury became the owner of the Chelsea factory, and six years afterwards of that of Bow. The influence of the migration of Chelsea workmen to Derby, and the removal thither, in 1784, of the moulds and patterns, may be traced in Derby productions subsequent to the year 1770 : the effect of the transference of the Bow artists, recipes and plant, has perhaps not been recognised by connoisseurs.

The first W. Duesbury (the name occurs in other forms, Duesbrie, for instance), died in 1786. His son William carried on the business alone until 1795, when he took into partnership Mr. Michael Kean, a miniature painter ; the second W. Duesbury died in the following year. A third proprietor of the same name continued the manufacture until 1815, when he leased the factory to Mr. Robert Bloor. in 1848 the original business finally ceased to exist. Just before this time a small new factory was started by one Locker, formerly manager of Mr. Bloor's works This second factory, after several changes in the proprietary, is still in existence, and has quite recently been much augmented and improved.

It is usual to distinguish the productions of the several periods of the Derby factory by the terms Derby, Chelsea-Derby, Crown-Derby, and Bloor-Derby. The mark, if any, of the first period—from the founding of the works until the purchase by Duesbury of the Chelsea factory—has not been ascertained. To the second period, 1769-1773, belongs the mark of an anchor in gold placed within and across the D of Derby or Duesbury, also gilt : a crown, having the bows carefully jewelled, was added to the D mark in 1773, the cross batons and dots being introduced, it is said, in 1782, although we believe they were used before that date. This more complex mark, as well as the crowned D, was enamelled in various colours, as well as painted in gold, at first blue being used, then purple or puce, then gold, then light brown, then green,[1] and lastly, black The mark in red belongs to a part at least of the Bloor period, 1815-1831. it has been observed that the crown of the later marks is without jewels on the bows. For a short period after the year 1795, when the second W

---

[1] The crowned D without the batons, in green, was, however, an early mark See Jermyn Street collection, J. 80

Duesbury was in partnership with the miniature painter, Mr. M. Kean, the D of the mark was combined with a K. On biscuit figures and vases the Derby mark was incised or impressed. It should be added that the Chelsea-Derby mark appears to have been used at Chelsea as well as at Derby, not only from 1769 to 1773, but also from 1773 until the final closing of the Chelsea works in 1784.

Chelsea-Derby, 1769-1784.

Crown-Derby, 1773-1782.

Crown-Derby, 1782-1831.

Duesbury and Kean, 1795.

Crown-Derby, late.

A late Crown-Derby mark consists of a black-letter 𝔇 surmounted by an angular crown; it is thumb-printed in red enamel.

The crossed swords of Dresden and the double L of Sèvres, both in under-glaze blue, were also employed at Derby.

The late Mr. John Haslem, of the Derby works, ascertained the names of many of the artists engaged there, and the dates at which they were employed. F. Duvivier (1769), P. Stephan (1770), and R. Askew (1772), are amongst the painters; and J. J. Spengler (1790), and W. J. Coffee (1791) amongst the modellers. Other names are Bornford, Complin, Pegg, and Withers. W.

Billingsley, whose name appears in connection with many other factories, was apprenticed in the Derby works so early as 1774. In 1794 he was at Pinxton, in 1800 at Mansfield, in 1802 at Torkesay; then he appears at Wirksworth. He was working at Worcester in 1808, in 1813 at Nantgarw near Pontypridd, and, later on, at Dillwyn's Swansea pottery. Then he returned to Nantgarw, remaining there until he migrated to Coalport in 1820.

Amongst the Derby china specimens in the museums of Jermyn Street and South Kensington there are many examples of the work of the above painters and modellers, and of other artists, such as J. Caulton, T. Steele, and M. Webster. In the former collection J 64 should be noted for its painting, by Askew, of a group of country children and of sheep taking refuge beneath a tree during a thunderstorm. The pieces J 71 and 71a are examples of flower-painting by W. Billingsley: J 72, a *compotier*, is thought to be the work of E. Withers, who preceded Billingsley as chief flower-painter at Derby. There are in all about ninety specimens of Chelsea-Derby and Derby porcelain in the Jermyn Street collection; amongst them will be found all the known marks of the fabrique, and examples of almost all its characteristic styles of decoration. A number scratched in the paste before firing, or else enamelled in colour, often occurs on the base of the pieces; it refers to the model of the vase or figure, or to the pattern of the decoration. In the South Kensington Museum there are twelve pieces of Chelsea-Derby, and fourteen of Crown-Derby, besides the good representative series of this porcelain in the Schreiber Gift.

In the case of specimens of Chelsea-Derby it is rarely ascertainable whether they were made at Chelsea or at Derby. Sometimes a suite of five vases and beakers occurs bearing the Chelsea-Derby mark upon four of the pieces, and the simple anchor of Chelsea upon the fifth. It may be stated generally that such pieces, particularly the vases, correspond in paste and style with the later productions of Chelsea, but are more severe, or rather, less rococo in character than the rich vases made at Chelsea by Sprimont, in fact they are more like the productions of Sèvres during the period 1756-1765. The illustration (Fig. 11) is of a vase of Chelsea-Derby in the Jones Bequest, South Kensington Museum.

The *compotier* (Fig 12) is probably of the same period.

The coloured porcelain statuettes of Derby may be considered next in order. Their manufacture continued for some time, beginning probably almost with the beginning of the factory and lasting well on into the present century. But the earliest marked statuettes are not, we think, earlier than about the year 1770. The well-known figure of Falstaff (Jermyn Street collection, J 49) belongs here. so do the two statuettes from the Schreiber collection of a girl and a boy with pet animals (Figs 21 and 22). Perhaps no more exquisite pieces of this type can be pointed out than a pair of figures (J 12 and J 13) in the Jermyn Street collection. They are 5½ inches high, are coloured and gilt richly, but not extravagantly, and show great skill in modelling. There is some exquisite lace-work on the dresses, such as is found upon old Dresden statuettes; and they bear an imitative Dresden mark—the crossed swords in blue under the glaze.

For another class of figures Derby was without a rival: the statuettes in white biscuit are often of a very high degree of excellence They belong to a period which may be said to have begun in 1770, and generally bear incised in the paste the Crown-Derby mark with the batons, dots, and script D: usually they have a number also. In the Jermyn Street collection is an exquisite example—a statuette of Diana (J 43), which we engrave (Fig 23) it is 6½ inches high. In the South Kensington Museum is a large biscuit figure of Mars, 20¾ inches in height (No. 840 '73). In the Schreiber Gift are two good groups of children. Mr. Willett lent to the Alexandra Palace Exhibition a magnificent statuette of Hebe no less than 30 inches high: his collection is rich in these biscuit figures.

FIG. 21.—DERBY: GIRL WITH LAMB. SCHREIBER COLLECTION.

FIG. 22.—DERBY: BOY WITH DOG. SCHREIBER COLLECTION.

FIG. 23.—DERBY: DIANA, STATUETTE IN WHITE BISCUIT. MUSEUM PRACTICAL GEOLOGY.

FIG. 24.—DERBY: COVERED CUP AND SAUCER. MUSEUM OF PRACTICAL GEOLOGY.

FIG. 25.—DERBY: PLATE, PAINTED BY ASKEW, WITH AMORINO IN PINK CAMAÏEU. MUSEUM OF PRACTICAL GEOLOGY.

The late Mr. Haslem was of opinion that these white biscuit porcelain figures, for which the Derby factory was famous, could not have been made before 1800. He based that opinion upon the alleged first use at that time of bones in porcelain by Spode. This unfortunate error about the date of the introduction of bones, which we have controverted elsewhere (see pp. 21 and 29), is further disproved by the occurrence of these very biscuit figures in the Derby auction catalogues of 1771 and 1773: a few quotations will be interesting, not the less so on account of the prices at which the pieces were then sold:—

April 17, 1771   Lot 5   A pair of small antique vases in biscuit, 2*l.* 2*s.*
  ,,   ,,   Lot 57. A set of curious antique Seasons, on pedestals, in biscuit, 3*l.* 15*s.*
  ,,   ,,   Lot 72. A pair of curious sitting figures, elegantly finish'd with lace, in biscuit, 3*l.* 5*s.*
  20   ,,   Lot 9   A group of three figures, Minerva crowning Constancy, and Hercules killing the hydra, with a pyramid in the middle, in biscuit, 3*l.* 9*s.*

February and March, 1773. In these sales there were figures in biscuit of the Muses, of Bacchus on a goat, and Cupid on a panther, and of the Virtues. There were also vases and beakers in the same ware.

In the sales of 1778, 1779, and 1780, various pieces in biscuit are named, although all the lots are attributed on the title pages of the catalogues to Chelsea. In some of the subsequent sales, however, the productions of Derby are again introduced by name.

Of the breakfast and dessert equipages made at Derby a few words must suffice. Our illustration (Fig. 24) represents a covered cup and saucer in Jermyn Street (J 24). The deep blue borders with gold leafage, and the simple festoons in pink, constituted a frequent and characteristic decoration of the early Crown-Derby period. So also did the "Chantilly sprig," and other simple conventional designs of leaves and flowers: these were executed sometimes in colours and sometimes in gold. Examples of this style, which belong to an early date of the works, are the following pieces in the Jermyn Street collection: J 42a, a cup and saucer with pale blue festoons; J 25, a fluted cup and saucer with gilt border; and J 34, a two-handled cup and stand, ornamented with broad canary-yellow band and blue chevron border with gilt wreath.

Attention should be drawn, amongst the examples of a more ornate and pictorial style, to the plate (J 67) with an amorino in pink camaieu in centre by Askew (Fig. 25), to the rich border in blue and gold of the plate, J 64; to the very beautiful paintings in natural colours of plants in bloom, placed upright round the coffee-can, J 36 (Fig. 26), and to the six pieces (J 40, 60, 60a, 60b, 60c, and 93) illustrating the chief "Japan" patterns in vogue at the Derby works during the last years of the eighteenth century and in the beginning of the present. These, like most of the finer pieces of the later time at Derby, were profusely decorated with rich gilding.

Little can be said as to the materials used in the Derby works previous to the year 1769: probably the early body was a frit porcelain containing Dorset clay: bones were afterwards used; and lastly, china clay and china stone. There is an earthiness or opacity about the paste of the later ware, especially during the Bloor period, which detracts from the quality of the enamel-colours used. The three vases or bottles, J 14, 15, 16, in Jermyn Street collection are, however, good examples of this late period. The gros-bleu and deep pink ground-colours are of peculiarly rich quality.

CHAPTER V.

WORCESTER.

Wall and Davis—Changes of ownership—Under- and over-glaze printing—Vases—Marks—Paste.

THE credit of originating Worcester porcelain must be shared between Dr. John Wall, physician, and Mr. William Davis, apothecary, both of the city of Worcester. This appears from the partnership deeds [1] or "articles for carrying on the Worcester Tonquin manufacture," which bear date the 4th of June, 1751, and disclose the names of fifteen partners, two of whom, named above, are described as possessing the secret, art, mystery, and process for making "porcellain." In this deed Wall and Davis are awarded five 100*l.* shares in the company in payment for their invention. The capital of the partners consisted of forty-five 100*l.* shares, thus contributed :—

	£	s.	d.		£	s.	d.
Dr. W. Bayliess	675	0	0	Dr. John Wall	225	0	0
Edward Cave	562	10	0	William Davis	225	0	0
Richard Holdship	562	10	0	Edward Jackson	225	0	0
Richard Brodribb	225	0	0	Samuel Bradley	225	0	0
John Brodribb }				John Doharty	225	0	0
John Berwick }	225	0	0	Samuel Pritchett	225	0	0
Josiah Holdship	450	0	0	William Oliver	112	10	0
John Thorneloe	337	10	0				

---

[1] Reprinted in 1883 by Mr. R. W. Binns, to whose kindness I am indebted for a copy.

From the partnership deeds we learn that two workmen, R. Podmore and John Lyes, who had been employed for some time by the inventors of the Worcester porcelain, were to receive extra remuneration, "the better to engage their fidelity to keep such part of the secret as may be intrusted to them." Precautions were also taken to prevent the entrance into the works of inquisitive visitors. No strangers were to be admitted into the factory, which was to be carried on with the greatest privacy and secrecy. Even the keys of the outer and inner doors were not to be kept by the same guardian. When the net profits of the works equalled 10 per cent. per annum, then a hundred pounds was to be divided between the joint inventors. The articles of partnership were for the term of twenty-one years It should be noted here that one of the joint inventors, W. Davis, practically managed the factory.

The Worcester porcelain works were established near St. Andrew's Church, and on the side of the river Severn. The building appropriated to the factory was a large mansion known as Warmstry House, at the time the property of a Mr. Evett. It had formerly belonged to Thomas, Lord Windsor, and is now part of Dent's glove factory. In August, 1752, a view of the porcelain manufactory at Worcester appeared in the *Gentleman's Magazine;* it was accompanied by a notice of the new venture. This wood-cut showed the "Biscuit Kilns," the "Glazing Kilns," the "Great Kiln for Seggars," the "Pressing and Modelling Gallery," and the "Rooms for Turning, Throwing, and Drying the Ware." The early appearance of this notice of the infant factory in the pages of the *Gentleman's Magazine* is explained by the fact that Edward Cave, the originator of that periodical, was one of the three chief proprietors and partners of the porcelain company.

After the death of Dr. Wall in 1776 the remaining members of the original company continued the manufacture until 1783, when they disposed of the works to their London agent

Mr. Flight. The chief subsequent changes are enumerated here :—

1783. Mr. Chamberlain set up new works (the present).
1793. Mr. Barr became a partner.
1840. Messrs. Flight and Barr joined with Messrs. Chamberlain.
1847. The partnership of 1840 dissolved and the original factory ceased.
1850. Mr. F. Lilly and Mr. Kerr became partners.
1852. Mr. Binns became a partner.
1862. Messrs. Kerr and Co. disposed of their business to the present Joint Stock Co.—" The Worcester Royal Porcelain Company, Limited."

The above changes, or at least some of them, are of interest from an artistic point of view, since they were often accompanied by a change in the style or "taste" of the productions of the factory. The early period, distinguished for its simplicity and for the prevalence of reproductions of Chinese and Japanese designs, began with the works, and terminated with the engagement of Chelsea painters in 1768. The second period, 1768 to 1783, covers the time during which the finest vases (often in the Dresden and Sèvres taste) turned out by the works were made. The third of the periods, which we may designate as old, began with the sale of the works to Mr. Flight in 1783, and closed in 1793 when Mr. Barr was taken into the partnership. The artistic decadence of the ware began during this period, although the potting and the workmanship remained excellent. But the heavy pseudo-classic forms, the laboured painting, and the exuberant gilding that were now in vogue, gradually displaced the last traces of the grace, freedom, and simplicity of the earlier time. The lavish use of gold, the ugly gadrooned edges to plates, the flat uninteresting colours, and the immense coats-of-arms which characterise the services produced during the later years of the eighteenth century and the beginning of the nineteenth, show

how well the painters and gilders could succeed in suppressing the higher elements of human handiwork, and in achieving results mechanically perfect, but the very prose of porcelain. The story is a common one. The fault is usually attributed to the changing fashions, and the lowering of the taste of the day. Happy, after all, was it for some china-factories that an untimely fate put an end to their existence before the degradation of their productions was complete. However extravagant and bizarre were the forms of some of the vases of Chelsea porcelain, they are not amenable to the charge of hardness in outline or mechanical precision in finish.

All the usual methods of decorating porcelain were employed at Worcester. The application of enamel colours by transfer-printing, both under and over the glaze, was very extensively used. The ordinary blue and white "printed Worcester" owes its excellence not merely to the fine quality of the porcelain body, but also to the skill shown in the form, decoration, and general style of the pieces. The accompanying woodcut (Fig. 27), which represents a cup of the usual blue under-glaze printed Worcester in the South Kensington Museum, illustrates the merits of these ordinary productions of the factory.

One of the modes of decorating porcelain for which Worcester became famous was that of transfer-printing *over* the glaze. The pieces so decorated are commonly tea-services, plates, bowls, mugs, and jugs. Usually the porcelain is thin and of very beautiful quality. The transfer is, as a rule, black, called in the old sale catalogues "jet enamell'd;" but a purplish lavender and a deep brick-red colour were also used. Some of the engraved copper-plates show not only fine workmanship, but a freedom and gracefulness which make the impressions taken from them, whether on porcelain or on paper, really beautiful as works of art. But two or three specimens of this over-glaze transfer-printed porcelain bear a mark [1] (for the simple reason that they never passed through

---

[1] The crossed swords with the figure 9 between the points are found on a cup in the collection at the Worcester works.

SOUTH KENSINGTON MUSEUM ART HANDBOOKS.

ENGLISH PORCELAIN.

PART II.

a painter's hands), save that in a part of the picture the initials or the name of the engraver occasionally appear. *R. Hancock fecit* and R. H. *Worcester*, sometimes are found separately or together; the latter mark, having the two letters as a monogram, and surmounted by an anchor, perhaps stands for Richard Holdship. In this connection it may be mentioned that when some verses, commendatory of Josiah Holdship, appeared in the *Gentleman's Magazine* for December, 1757, the *Worcester Journal*, in reprinting them in the following January, added the following couplet:—

" Hancock, my friend, don't grieve tho' Holdship has the praise,
'Tis yours to execute, 'tis his to wear the bays."

Hancock was in truth the engraver; the two Holdships, Josiah and Richard, owned between them one-fourth of the capital of the porcelain company.

The accompanying illustration (Fig. 28) shows this style of decoration in transfer-printing over the glaze. The portrait is that of the Marquis of Granby. The most popular of these engravings was, however, that of Frederick the Great; it is found, accompanied by figures of Fame and military trophies, on mugs, jugs, cups, plates, &c., and occurs in several sizes. The date of these pieces is 1757. A less common print was one of George II., with ships, emblems, and the inscription "Liberty." "A Tea-party," "Ruins," "Courtship," "Milkmaids in a Farmyard," "Birds," "Swans," "Chinese Groups," and "The Hunt," are other well-known subjects of these engravings. A print from Roubiliac's statue of Shakespeare, with figures of Tragedy and Comedy, is found upon a mug in the collection at the Worcester factory. Engravings after pictures by Watteau, Le Rat, Gainsborough, and other artists also occur on Worcester porcelain.

A good many specimens of the transfer-prints of landscapes, ruins, figures, &c., were further decorated with enamel-colours added by hand. Generally these examples cannot be considered successful in their artistic effect; but there are exceptions.

Attention may be directed in this connection to the fine hexagonal vase in the Schreiber collection shown in Fig. 29. The panels, reserved in white on a clear canary-yellow enamelled ground, are decorated with transfer-prints, in black, of ruins and trees; these views are further enamelled by hand in colours

Transfer-printing appears to have been first practised on enamel at Battersea by Alderman Sir S T. Janssen (Lord Mayor of London in 1754); then on delft and earthenware at Liverpool by Sadler and Green; then on porcelain at Worcester, Bow, Chelsea, Caughley, Derby, and Bristol. The same process was used for the decoration of fine white salt-glazed stoneware at Burslem. But this method attained the greatest perfection at Worcester, and was there more extensively used than at other manufactories of earthenware and porcelain for the adornment of the best work.

After all, the renown of Worcester porcelain will always be mainly founded upon its vases and shaped pieces, hand-painted in enamel colours, and judiciously decorated with gilding. The ground colours of such vases, dishes, baskets, &c., are even, without being flat and monotonous. Five of these hues are well known—a deep or mazarine blue, sometimes "*gros bleu,*" sometimes "powdered," and sometimes marked with the salmon-scale pattern; a fine turquoise blue; a pea or camellia leaf green; a maroon, and a canary yellow. On the spaces or panels, reserved in white, exotic or tropical birds and flowers were painted in rich colours, the outlines being pencilled with a firm yet free hand in a darkish tint of grey or brown. The style was a happy mean between exact realism and hard conventionalism, shadows and shading being in great measure ignored. When the designs were inclosed in panels, a framework of gilding in the form of scrolls generally bordered the paintings; the gilding, both matt and burnished, especially after the first few years, was rich in substance and colour. The designs of tropical birds, flowers, and butterflies, were continued to a very late period of the factory; but the excellence of the enamels, of the drawing, of the touch, did not

FIG. 29.—WORCESTER: VASE, YELLOW GROUND, PAINTED AND PRINTED.
SCHREIBER COLLECTION.

FIG. 27.—WORCESTER: COFFEE-CUP, PRINTED IN UNDERGLAZE BLUE.
SOUTH KENSINGTON MUSEUM. NO. 3215, '53.

Fig. 28.—WORCESTER: MUG, TRANSFER PRINTED IN BLACK. SCHREIBER COLLECTION.

FIG. 26.—DERBY: COFFEE CAN. MUSEUM OF PRACTICAL GEOLOGY.

FIG. 30.—WORCESTER: VASE, PAINTED WITH TROPICAL BIRDS.
SCHREIBER COLLECTION.

last much, if at all, longer than the close of the best period of the manufacture, about the year 1783. The opening of that period may be traced, we think, to the engagement in 1768 of a number of enamel painters from Chelsea. This migration to Worcester of several trained artists was attended with favourable results; but it of necessity resulted in a certain degree of resemblance between the productions of Chelsea and Worcester. In Worcester, however, the remnants of the Chinese traditional ornament and form not only modified the style and design imported from Chelsea, but restrained the exuberance and bizarrerie which were so conspicuous in the last few years of that factory. A magnificent vase in the Schreiber collection (Fig. 30) illustrates at once the blue salmon-scale ground, the rich gilt bordering, and the tropical birds, to which attention has been drawn in the preceding paragraph.

Besides the designs we have already named, the Chinese figure subjects, horsemen, peasants, animals, shells and landscapes, are found beautifully painted upon some of the pieces of the best period. The names of Donaldson, O'Neale, and C. C. Fogo, occur amongst the enamellers of such pieces. But a good deal of the Worcester porcelain before 1768 must have been enamelled and gilt in London—at least so we conclude from an advertisement of J. Giles in 1768 to this effect. It is evident that the manager at Worcester had nothing whatever to do with decorations so applied, and that a great variety of designs, and probably much inferior painting as well, were most likely applied to the ware under such conditions. No doubt, even at Worcester itself, as indeed in all other extensive works, the individuality of certain artists of unusual power asserted itself in unusual ways. For example, there is, in the collection at Worcester, a large mug (of the harder body not infrequently made at Worcester) which, both in marks and decoration, suggests a special origin. It may have been decorated by R. Holdship at home. It bears in red a mark which seems to be the figure 9 followed by an anchor. The decoration consists of flowers and Chinese figures, the enamel colours in which these are painted having been laid on with great freedom, and producing a flooded appearance not usually met with on old Worcester porcelain. A smaller mug of similar paste has a red mark (of an arrow with an annulet and a bar) which has been erroneously attributed to Bow.

Some resemblances between the productions of Caughley and Worcester have been often noticed. The notion that Worcester porcelain was ever printed or decorated at Caughley seems to us preposterous. The more probable explanation of the occurrence of similar or identical transfer-prints and enamelled decorations upon the wares of these two factories seems to lie in the following circumstance: When, in 1783, the Messrs Chamberlain left the original Worcester China Works in order to found an establishment of their own, they were not at first able to make their own porcelain, but procured it from Caughley, decorating it, of course, with the same designs and colours as they had been accustomed to use in the original factory.

There is one beautiful enamel-colour, painted over the glaze, which is peculiar to Worcester amongst the English china factories of the eighteenth century. It is a brilliant and intense lapis-lazuli blue, derived from cobalt. Its surface is nearly matt. The decorations painted with it are floral sprays somewhat conventionally treated. Mr. Nightingale has a fine globular vase and cover, sixteen inches high, with festoons of these bright blue flowers on a white ground, and further ornamented with applied flowers in full relief and with perforations. In the Museum of Practical Geology there is a tea jar which shows the style usually adopted for these blue-painted pieces, although in this case the colour is red-purple, and there are gilt scroll-borders to two of the floral sprays. This jar (Fig. 31) is, moreover, an excellent example of the graceful yet simple forms prevalent in the best period of the Worcester Works.

One of the most popular of all the ornamental pieces made in English china factories during the last century is the "shell centre-

FIG. 31.—WORCESTER: TEA-JAR, PAINTED AND GILT.   MUSEUM OF
PRACTICAL GEOLOGY.

FIG. 32.—WORCESTER: CENTRE PIECE OF SHELL WORK, PAINTED WITH COLOURS, AND TOUCHED WITH GOLD. MR. J. E. NIGHTINGALE'S COLLECTION.

piece," or *compotier*, for the dessert table. It consisted of from one to five tiers of scallops, embedded in a mass of rockwork, shells, and seaweed, and was produced at Bow, Chelsea, and Bristol, as well as at Worcester. A very fine example is in Mr Nightingale's collection at Wilton. This has the scallops edged with a broad band of blue, and painted with flowers, while the shells of the rockwork are delicately touched with gold (see Fig. 32)

Of the numerous forms of vases and of tea and dessert services made at Worcester during the best time there is no space here for any description. Reference may, however, be made to the Schreiber collection for actual examples, and to such works as Mr. R. W. Binns' *A Century of Pottery in the City of Worcester*, and *A Catalogue of the Collection of Worcester Porcelain at Worcester*, for woodcuts and descriptions The decoration of the pieces depends so much upon the quality and handling of the colours, that neither woodcuts nor descriptions can do it adequate justice But mention must be made of the ingenious adaptations of oriental designs, both in form and in painted ornament, to this English ware. So close, for instance, was the imitation of Chinese figures, that nothing indicates their European workmanship save a slight difference in the pencilling of the eyelids and eyebrows The plates, with white panels painted with flowers on a powder blue ground, and the rich patterns of "mosaic Japan" on mugs and vases, afford excellent examples of success in the reproduction of oriental designs.

There is a style of impressed ornament carried to great perfection at Worcester about which a word should be said. Flutings and ribbings, the pine-cone, the artichoke, the trellis, the diaper, and many another pressed pattern were employed as decorative motives in other factories as well as at Worcester; but to the latter workshop must be assigned the credit of producing (or, shall we say, reproducing?) exquisite and minute floral ornaments *in the paste*, similar to those which are met with on some old pieces of white Chinese egg-shell porcelain. An illustration from the author's collection (Fig. 33) fails to convey the peculiar delicacy of the patterns, which need, in order to be fully revealed, a strong beam of transmitted light.

The marks on old Worcester porcelain are of two sorts, factory marks and workmen's marks. The crescent, the Chinese square, and the letter *W*, belong to the former series. To the latter must be assigned a crowd of small signs, made up of letters, lines, dots, circles, &c., which are the marks of individual enamellers and gilders. At least seventy of the last-named group of marks have been recorded for the old Worcester period, 1751-1783, and there are a great many on the later wares made at the rival factory set up in 1783 by Messrs. Chamberlain, and also on the pieces turned out from the original factory after 1793 until 1840. It is impossible to give precedence in order of date to the three best known of the early factory marks—for they now and then occur, or two of them occur, together on the same piece. The open crescent is usually in blue under the glaze; sometimes, but very rarely, in over-glaze red; a few examples in gold are known; it is of various sizes. The solid or ruled crescent is generally found upon pieces printed in blue under the glaze. A capital E is sometimes placed in the hollow of the crescents. Of the *W* mark five or six varieties have been noted; they are in blue under-glaze, and are generally of fairly large size, though they are not always so. The oriental fretted square is really a copy of a mark imitating a Chinese seal-character, and found on blue and white porcelain of good quality, but made, it is thought, for the European market. Connoisseurs are divided in opinion as to whether it is Chinese or Japanese. The Worcester copies include four or five varieties, none of which are identical with the original form; the two given in the margin are those of commonest occurrence. Besides the above-named factory marks. the same value must be given

FIG. 33.—WORCESTER: TEACUP, VERY THIN WITH EMBOSSED PATTERN. CHURCH COLLECTION.

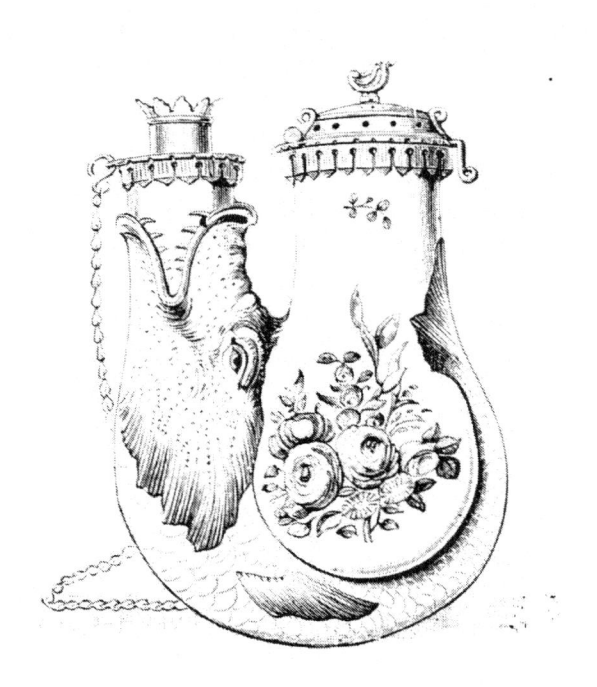

FIG. 34.—WORCESTER: BOWL OF TOBACCO PIPE. SCHREIBER COLLECTION.

to certain imitative Chinese marks made up of four or six disguised numerals and letters; also to imitative Dresden marks, such as the cross-swords with the figure 9 or 91 between the points.

The marks above described belong essentially to the original Worcester fabrique from its beginning until the year 1783, when the surviving members of the Company sold their property to a Mr. Flight, their London agent. The marks of the years 1783 to 1793 consisted of the name FLIGHTS, or Flight, or the latter surmounted by a crown. Afterwards, the names or initials of the members of the firm subsequent to 1793 were given, sometimes painted, and sometimes impressed in the paste. Amongst these marks of the later period occur *Flight & Barr*, *Flight Barr & Barr*, BARR, FLIGHT & BARR, FBB, and BFB. These marks are occasionally surmounted by a regal crown.

The wares of the Messrs. Chamberlain (1786 to 1852) were marked with their name, sometimes simply in the form *Chamberlain's;* their London address was generally added. The present flourishing Worcester Royal Porcelain Works Company really represents, not the original factory of Dr. Wall, but the offshoot founded by the Messrs. Chamberlain. Its productions are of very commendable beauty and variety.

The constituents or composition of Worcester porcelain must claim a moment's attention. Three pastes or bodies were used at different times at Worcester; in all a glassy frit was first prepared by heat; and then a certain proportion of this frit was ground up and mixed with other materials, mainly of an infusible sort. Amongst these the "hard or soft soapy rock" of Cornwall, a kind of impure steatite from near Mullion, took an important place. Another paste was made by adding whiting and pipeclay to the glassy frit; a third paste by the use of bone-ash. All these varieties of material, with ground flint and several other materials employed in smaller proportions, were used in the earlier period of the works; even the introduction of bone-ash probably took place within the first decade of their foundation.

In the year 1765 Holdship received a box of true China clay from the Cherokee territory, doubtless the same material and from the same locality as the clay called unaker, named in the Bow China patent of 1744. Holdship appreciated the clay, and asked for more of it, but there is no proof that this or any other kaolin was used in any of the Worcester productions until many years after the year 1765

The varieties of bodies used at Worcester accounts for the great differences in hardness and in other qualities often noticed in the wares of this factory. The frit used at Worcester had a little smalt in it to correct the yellow colour which would have arisen from the iron present as impurity in the sand and other ingredients, this causes the cool greenish hue observed on looking through a bit of old white Worcester. The glaze on the ware, though rather hard, contained a considerable proportion of lead.

It is generally considered that statuettes were never made at Worcester. However, a pair of fine figures marked with the Worcester crescent in blue have lately been discovered in an old country mansion; their paste and style of colouring are such as to leave little doubt that they were made at the Worcester works during the latter part of the Wall period.

A word about the prices of old Worcester porcelain may interest collectors. Thanks to Mr. Nightingale's reprint of an old sale catalogue of Worcester productions (1769) we are enabled to compare the auction prices of a century or more back with those of to-day. At the sale just named a dessert-service, "jet enamelled," numbering twenty-five pieces, brought 28s.; forty-three pieces, constituting a complete tea and coffee equipage of the "fine old Japan star pattern," were sold for 71s., a suite of three hexagon jars and covers of mazarine blue with gold, enamelled in birds and insects, realized 8*l.* 15*s* These three lots would have fetched in 1874 more pounds than they did shillings in 1769 And even now (1884), when Old English porcelain does not bring quite such extravagant prices, a fine suite of three vases with tropical birds could not be bought for less than 150*l.* to 200*l.*

In the Schreiber collection is a piece of English porcelain of unusual form which has been attributed to Worcester. It is the bowl of a tobacco pipe : it is shown in Fig 34

CHAPTER VI

PLYMOUTH.

Cookworthy—Short duration of Works—Marks.

THE true china clay or kaolin was first discovered and identified in England by William Cookworthy, about the year 1755. Cookworthy (a member of the Society of Friends) was born at Kingsbridge, Devonshire, on the 5th of April 1705 he died at Plymouth on the 17th of October 1780. He was a wholesale chemist and druggist and a man of good education, great intelligence, and keen powers of observation. His business frequently took him into the china-clay districts of Cornwall. His attention had been directed to the subject of kaolin and pe-tun-tse in the year 1745 by an American Quaker, but it was not until several years afterwards that Cookworthy discovered both china clay and china stone in Tregonning hill, and then near Breage in St Stephen's and in Boconnoc. He recognised with perfect accuracy the differences in aspect and properties between the infusible clay and the fusible felspathic stone, and made many experiments with these two ingredients of true china, using both in several different proportions for the body or paste of his porcelain, and the stone alone, or mixed with lime and potash, for the glaze. Cookworthy was also familiar with the process of dipping the "raw" or unfired ware into the glazing materials and then burning the vessels in one firing, although his finer productions were biscuited—that is, the body was burnt before it was painted or glazed. We learn also, from a memorandum which he wrote on the subject, that he used wood as the fuel for his kilns, and that the latter were similar to those employed for stoneware. The date of this memorandum is not precisely known, but it was probably written several years prior to 1768. That Cookworthy had made trials of Cornish china-stone even before 1758 is clear from Borlase's statement in that year on this subject. The actual foundation of the Plymouth porcelain works cannot however be placed earlier than the year 1768, the date of Cookworthy's patent, which was granted on the 17th of March in that year. The manufacture was supported by the pecuniary help of Thomas Pitt of Boconnoc, afterwards created (in 1784) Lord Camelford. The china works were situated at Coxside, Plymouth, the owners securing the artistic aid of a French painter, one Soqui or Sequoi, for the correct spelling of his name is not known. Bone, afterwards well known for his enamels on copper, was not employed by Cookworthy but by Champion at Bristol. The Plymouth works do not seem to have been carried on for more than three years, since we find that "Messrs. Cookworthy and Co" had a china factory at Bristol from 1771 to 1773 on premises now known as No. 15, Castle Green. In the autumn of the last-named year, Richard Champion, who had been experimenting in porcelain-making since 1765, bought Cookworthy's patent and other rights, the legal transfer being completed in the spring of 1774. From September 1773 until March 1782 this china factory was in the occupation of Richard Champion. We have said above that W. Cookworthy and Co's works were transferred to Bristol not later than 1771; it is possible that they may have been removed from Plymouth in the preceding year; for in the *Worcester Journal* of 22nd March, 1770, there appeared an advertisement for "a number of sober artists capable of painting in enamel or blue" wanted by "the Plymouth New Invented Porcelain Manufactory." It is difficult to suppose the works were then at Plymouth, for if so, why should applicants be invited to communicate with T. Frank of Castle Street, Bristol? But if the works were just then being moved from Plymouth to Bristol, such a direction would be quite natural.

If our views be correct, then it must be held that the manufacture of porcelain at Plymouth was never pushed to any very high degree of perfection nor carried on to any large extent. So it is extremely probable that several vases and other highly decorated specimens of hard paste porcelain bearing the Plymouth mark but of much finer quality than anything known or likely to have been made at Plymouth, were really the product of the Bristol works after Champion had acquired Cookworthy's patent. The mark, the symbol for tin, was doubtless used, instead of (sometimes associated with) the cross of Bristol to indicate the origin of the manufacture and of the characteristic materials from Cornwall, the land of tin, used in it. But, although Champion is known to have made enamelled hard porcelain several years before the transference to him of Cookworthy's rights in 1773—witness his memoranda about his enamel kiln in 1770—it is pretty certain that he would not use the mark employed by Cookworthy until he had acquired the full right to do so. Mr. Hugh Owen (*op. cit.* p. 25) has cleared up the difficulty. He concludes that Champion worked the patent at first under a license from Cookworthy probably as early as 1768, and that it was not until some time in the year 1770 that the Plymouth works were abandoned and transferred to Bristol in their entirety; the interest in them of Champion and his partners becoming complete in 1773. Champion and Cookworthy had been in friendly communication with each other since 1764, and so we may accept the confirmation of our opinion as to the productions of the Plymouth factory afforded by Champion's evidence before Parliament in the year 1774. Even at that time Champion described his own porcelain as "an *almost* perfect manufacture,"

FIG. 35.—PLYMOUTH; SALT-CELLAR, WHITE SHELLWORK. MUSEUM OF PRACTICAL GEOLOGY.

while he characterises that of Cookworthy as "very imperfect." He also states that he had been concerned in Cookworthy's undertaking nearly from the time the patent was granted to Cookworthy. Taking all the available evidence as a whole it must be concluded that many pieces of porcelain bearing the Plymouth mark, such as the lapis-lazuli tea-pot and coffee-pot now in the Schreiber collection but once in that of the Cookworthy family, and a fine vase in the Francis Fry collection from the same source, and similarly marked, are productions of the Bristol and not of the Plymouth works. But there are still a fair number of specimens in public collections which we may point to as undoubted specimens of Cookworthy's porcelain made at Plymouth. The Jermyn Street Museum is rich in these Amongst undoubted early pieces we would name—a mug with gilt chevron border (K9) and painted with coloured flowers: it bears the Plymouth mark in brown: a tea-cup (K18), painted with conventional foliage in blackish blue and marked under the glaze with the same colour: a plate (K16) painted in dull blue under the glaze and also marked; and an unmarked tea-cup enamelled with flowers in red, yellow, and green, over the glaze. All these pieces are glazed with the same dull-hued thick glaze as that found upon the three uncoloured statuettes (K3, 4, 5) in the same collection, and upon the pair of shell salt-cellars (K1 and K2) figure 35 The glaze on these figures is clearly produced mainly by a felspathic material, that is, as we know from Cookworthy's records of his experiments, by a china-stone or growan-stone rich in felspar. The glaze is too thick and insufficiently fired Cookworthy was aware of these defects He says, with reference to his process of glazing, "we first baked our ware to a soft biscuit which would suck, then painted it with blue and dipped it . . . But the proper thickness of the glaze is not so easily distinguished in this way," as when the ware is thoroughly burnt first so as to be non-absorbent. And he speaks, in another place, of the vapours of the fuel tingeing the surface of the ware.

and of the grey colour which the glazing material exhibited when insufficiently fired. It may be as well here to add that Cookworthy used for his glaze one part of slaked lime and two parts of fern ashes fritted together, and then he took for one part of his frit from ten to twenty of china-stone, fifteen parts being a very suitable proportion. He adds that for the body of his porcelain he generally employed equal parts of washed kaolin and washed pe-tun-tse; in his specification he named other proportions as well.

In the South Kensington Museum are four shell salt-cellars (209 to 212 '66), besides the fine series of Plymouth specimens belonging to the Schreiber collection.

We do not know whether Cookworthy's porcelain factory at Plymouth was in any way connected with the delft works at that place. This delft was often excellent in its opaque enamel (see K21 in the Jermyn Street collection), while its flower-painting sometimes resembled that on the hard porcelain.

One mark only belongs to the Plymouth factory, namely the alchemist's sign for tin (Jupiter), which resembles the Arabic numerals 2 and 4 conjoined. It is found in blue under the glaze, and in a brown over-glaze enamel upon early pieces undoubtedly made at Plymouth. The great majority of the pieces bearing the same mark in gold were made at Bristol. The forms which the mark assumed in the hands of the different Plymouth painters did not differ much from each other: we give two examples.

The discovery of china-clay in Cornwall by Cookworthy is placed between the years 1745 and 1750 by Mr. R N. Worth. This writer, in the *Transactions of the Devon Association for the Advancement of Science, Literature, and Art*, published in 1876 some notes concerning the manufacture of porcelain at Plymouth and Bristol. He concludes that Cookworthy began a factory at Bristol before January 1764, but had given it up by February 1766.

He also considers that Cookworthy made porcelain at Plymouth before the date, March 17th, 1768, of his patent. He regards all porcelain bearing the mark of the symbol for tin as having been made by Cookworthy at Plymouth. If this view be confirmed, the family tradition, which assigned such choice pieces as the tea-pot (Fig. 42) and the coffee-pot of the same set, in the Schreiber collection, to Plymouth, would, after all, be correct.

CHAPTER VII.

BRISTOL.

Richard Champion—Advertisements and Auctions—Apprentices—Champion and Cookworthy—Champion and Wedgwood—Presentation tea sets—Flower-plaques, vases, and figures—Prices of Bristol Porcelain—Marks

IF we may trust some very strong traditional evidence, a rough sort of porcelain must have been made in Bristol as early as the year 1753. John Britain or Brittan, afterwards foreman in Richard Champion's Bristol china factory, gave to his sister a plate, made and painted by himself, and bearing the above date and the initials J B. This plate, as well as a bowl dated 1762 with the initials F B, and the blacksmiths' arms (John Brittan's brother, an ironmonger, was named Francis), are of a rough, thick, and hard porcelain, and are both painted in the same Chinese style A second trial of porcelain-making in Bristol is mentioned incidentally by Champion, who wrote, in February 1766, that he had made some experiments on the employment of South Carolina clay in a china manufactory in Bristol, which, having been unsuccessful, was given up This second attempt at porcelain-making must have had a very brief existence. It was "just established" on the 7th November 1765, and was spoken of on the 15th December in the same year as "just given up." It does not seem to have been connected with the foundation of Champion's later factory. The final result of the inquiries made as to Champion's own manufacture of hard porcelain is to place

FIG. 36.—PLYMOUTH: "ASIA." SCHREIBER COLLECTION.

its date sometime during the year 1768, but the position of the works in Bristol has not been ascertained. Sometime after February and before September 1770, W Cookworthy removed his Plymouth factory to (what is now) No. 15, Castle Green, Bristol. Champion, who had previously, we believe, been working under a license from Cookworthy, may now have become more intimately interested in these porcelain works: we know that he bought the entire patent right in 1773, the transfer being completed legally in the following year. Further particulars concerning this transference will be found in the chapter on Plymouth Porcelain p 57. From 1773 until 1781 Champion was owner of the Castle Green factory, and carried on his manufacture there. Before this time, by the aid of friends, he had obtained the capital necessary to start the works. The exact amount of this, at first (in 1768) is not known, but it was probably at least 5,000*l*, of which a Mr. Joseph Harford contributed no less than 3,000*l*, and one E. Brice, 1,000*l*. Later on, Mr. Joseph Fry placed 1,500*l*. in the business, and Mr. Thomas Frank 1,000*l*. That a considerable amount of china had been made before Champion bought the patent of Cookworthy is evident from sale advertisements in the Bristol papers. On March 30th, 1771, an advertisement, in *Felix Farley's Journal*, mentioned " some beautiful dessert services, ornamental figures, candlesticks, and many other valuable articles of the Bristol manufactury, which will be sold by retail at Taylor's Hall." In August 1772, a sale by auction is announced of useful and ornamental china, the produce of the Bristol manufactory. In this sale were included "very elegant figures, beautiful vases, jars, and beakers, with all kinds of useful china, blue and white, and enamelled " On the 28th November, 1772, a still more interesting announcement appeared in Sarah Farley's *Bristol Journal*. This later advertisement described the Bristol porcelain as "wholly free from the imperfections in wearing which the English china usually has, and its composition as equal in fineness to the East Indian, and will wear as well. The enamelled ware, which is rendered nearly as cheap as the English blue and white comes very near, and, in some pieces, equals the Dresden, which this work more particularly imitates." The information here furnished is of particular value as confirming the conclusions derived from the study of many specimens of Bristol china. Not only do these follow the forms and decoration of Dresden porcelain, but they frequently bear the characteristic Dresden mark, the crossed swords, in under-glaze blue. Sometimes, it is true, this imitative Dresden mark was subsequently concealed by the distinctive Bristol marks of the letter B, or of a cross followed by a number, painted over the glaze. This concealment of the imitation Dresden mark (which indeed must be characterised we fear as a forgery) is not difficult to explain, but it has led writers on English porcelain so far astray that they have stated that Dresden china was decorated at Bristol. However, this compliment to Dresden paid by Champion was returned in kind, one hundred years afterwards, by a German china factory, from which emanated a number of forgeries of old Bristol china, duly marked with the Bristol cross. These pieces, mostly cups and saucers, first appeared about the year 1874 and were well calculated, from their paste, glaze, and decoration, to deceive even connoisseurs.

The history of the Bristol porcelain factory, from its foundation in 1768 to its abandonment in 1781, has been traced with exhaustive patience by Mr. Hugh Owen in his magnificent monograph, *Two Centuries of Ceramic Art in Bristol*. Mr Nightingale has since gleaned a few particulars concerning these works from the newspapers of the time. The limits of our space forbid us from giving in this place more than the barest outline of the operations and close of the factory.

Before the purchase of Cookworthy's patent in the autumn of 1773, Champion took at least seven apprentices as china-painters. Amongst these, the first in point of time was Henry Bone, afterwards known as a miniature painter and an enameller of great excellence. His mark was probably the figure 1, while the second

Fig. 37.—PLYMOUTH: "AMERICA." Schreiber Collection.

apprentice, W. Stephens, is known to have signed his work with the figure 2. It would seem that the eighteenth and last apprentice was indentured in July 1778. Trained painters and modellers were also engaged by Champion, but our information about them is too imperfect to be of any value.

Champion, in February 1775, presented a petition to Parliament for an extension of Cookworthy's patent for a further term of fourteen years beyond the original fourteen. After encountering great difficulties, chief amongst which was the serious opposition of the Staffordshire earthenware makers, headed by Josiah Wedgwood, an Act of Parliament was passed and received the royal assent in due course. Wedgwood's opposition was marked by bitterness and unfairness; it was moreover inconsistent with his own conduct and his expressed opinions with regard to inventions of his own. Champion's considerable labours and great outlay would now appear to have been likely to meet their reward. But unfortunately the public did not appreciate the superiority for practical purposes of hard paste over soft paste china, nor was a ready and remunerative sale obtained for the more richly decorated ornamental pieces. The Whig politics of Champion, and the time and toil he gave to political questions, were moreover undoubtedly adverse to the pecuniary success of his manufacture. Possibly, if he had devoted himself, at an earlier period of his labours, to the production on a larger scale of the simply decorated blue and white, and other cottage china (of hard paste, but burnt at a single firing) which he afterwards made, the factory might have enjoyed a longer and more prosperous life. As it happened, Bristol porcelain never secured that fashionable patronage which, unintelligent as some of it was, did so much for the productions of Chelsea and Worcester. It is not unlikely that the large and very sumptuous vases of Bristol china which are now extant were made partly as show-pieces and partly for those friends who had helped to start the works. Some small but choice specimens were made for exhibition to the Committee of the Commons before which

Champion's bill was discussed, and there remain some very beautiful presentation services. The most celebrated of these was a tea-set, a joint gift from Mr and Mrs Champion to Mrs. Edmund Burke. The pieces are marked with the usual cross and what appears to be a date—August 1st. It was given in 1774. The covers of this service have wreaths or groups of flowers in white biscuit; the painting on the larger pieces includes figures of Liberty and Plenty as supporters of a shield on which are the arms of Burke impaling Nugent: an inscription on each piece describes the present as a *pignus amicitiae*. When this service was dispersed by auction in 1871, the tea pot sold for 190*l*., and was subsequently purchased by a private collector for 210*l*. Another service made about the same time was of more refined decoration than that just mentioned. It was given by Edmund Burke to a Bristol merchant, Joseph Smith, at whose house Burke stayed when a candidate for Bristol in 1774. Mr. Smith's daughter presented a cup and saucer of this service to the South Kensington Museum (No 8,122 '62). Some very choice pieces of another tea-service are still in existence; they are decorated with exquisitely painted heads in *camaieu*-grey, on a maroon ground. Other productions of the best period of the Bristol factory, 1774-1778, were the plaques in white biscuit, having floral wreaths in full relief surrounding coats of arms or profile portraits. Of these, and of the fine vases and sets of statuettes, in which Champion's works attained a rare degree of excellence, something more will be said later on. Now it will suffice to remark that neither the finest plaques nor the finest vases appear to have been made for public sale.

We approach now a time when Champion began to despair of making a pecuniary success of his factory. His last appeal for the patronage of the public was made. In October 1779 his eldest daughter died. He commemorated his loss by means of a symbolic figure of Grief leaning on an urn. This piece of porcelain is the last dated work by Champion. The original statuette belongs to Mr. J. M. Desaussure of Camden, South

Carolina, who married a granddaughter of Champion, an uncoloured duplicate of this piece was sold at Christie's a few years ago. Shortly after, or probably even during this year 1779, Champion sought to dispose of his patent. He did so in 1781, to a company of seven Staffordshire potters, who originated the hard porcelain works at New Hall, Shelton. Champion's London warehouse, 17, Salisbury Court, Fleet Street, however, remained open until 1782 if not later. The remaining stock of china at the Bristol works was sold there by auction in May 1782 Champion left England on the 7th October, 1784, and settled on a farm called "Rocky Branch," in South Carolina. He died on the 7th October, 1791, in his forty-eighth year

The most characteristic productions of the Bristol factory were oval or round plaques, of white biscuit porcelain decorated with flowers and foliage, also of biscuit, in full relief applied to the surface. Some of these pieces were discs of comparatively small size, about $3\frac{1}{2}$ inches across, and having a single group of flowers in the middle. Others, still more finely wrought, were of larger dimensions, generally ovals six inches by five, bearing a shield of arms in the centre surrounded by wreaths and sprays of foliage. Amongst these armorial plaques, Mr. Hugh Owen records three bearing respectively the arms of France, of Elton impaling Tierney, and of Harford impaling Lloyd. A plaque with a bas-relief bust of Franklin measured $8\frac{3}{4}$ by $7\frac{1}{8}$ inches The finest steel engraving is inadequate to represent the exquisite tenuity and delicacy of these floral enrichments, which constitute the most marvellous triumphs of ceramic skill which have ever been produced in this style of ornament; they are far finer than the biscuit flowers made at Derby. Fragile, indeed, they were, but owing to the hardness and refractoriness of the paste, they passed without injury through such a fiery ordeal as that of the Alexandra Palace conflagration, which reduced the soft and fusible china of other English factories into shapeless lumps.

The best statuettes made at Bristol were modelled by an artist who seems to have worked for other potteries. His pieces are sometimes marked *To*, possibly a contraction for his name Tebo The Four Elements, figures ten inches high, were his work. Of the Seasons, a set of four statuettes eleven inches high, we engrave (Fig 38) the *Winter*, a boy skating. Another set of the Seasons is modelled in a severer and less modern style, but has less vitality. Other sets of Bristol figures, and single statuettes, some no less than fourteen inches high, have been met with, but they are rare. The coloured decoration on those specimens of Bristol figures which were not left in the white, was less elaborate than that adopted at Chelsea and at Derby at the same time The glitter of the glaze and cold hue of the porcelain detract, however, somewhat from the good workmanship of most of the extant Bristol statuettes. Illustrations of the style of the rarer types of these figures are furnished by the Figs. 39 and 40, which represent a boy with a hurdy-gurdy and a girl with a triangle; both pieces are in the Schreiber collection.

A few words must be said here concerning the fine hexagonal vases made at Bristol. They are about one foot high, or, including the cover, sixteen inches. Some have a neck of open or perforated work. They very rarely have coloured or salmon-scale grounds, but are enamelled with large trees in blue or green, with exotic birds, and occasionally a couple of large sprays of foliage and flowers in place of handles. The form of the vases and the style of the painting are good. The illustration (Fig. 41) is from a characteristic specimen in the Schreiber collection. Other fine vases are in the possession of Mr. F. Fry.

Thanks to Mr. J. E. Nightingale, who has reprinted a priced catalogue of a sale of Bristol porcelain held in 1780, an opportunity is afforded to us of comparing the values set upon this ware 100 years ago with those of the present day. On February 28th, 1780, two small circular flower medallions fetched 28s.; in 1875, a single one of the same character realised 10l. In 1874 an unusually large and fine specimen, perhaps the finest ever made, brought

FIG. 38.—BRISTOL: WINTER, A BOY SKATING. SCHREIBER COLLECTION.

FIG. 39.—BRISTOL: BOY WITH HURDY-GURDY. SCHREIBER COLLECTION.

FIG. 40.—BRISTOL: GIRL WITH TRIANGLE. SCHREIBER COLLECTION.

165*l*. It bore a bust of Franklin surrounded by a wreath of most delicately modelled flowers. In 1780 a "green festoon set of thirty-seven pieces," was sold for 36*s*.; nowadays it would fetch nearly twice as many pounds Jugs which realise from 12*l*. to 40*l* apiece now were sold in 1780 for 6*s*. 6*d*. apiece. "A fine ribbon-pattern dessert set with festoons of flowers, thirty-eight pieces," brought 15*l* 4*s*. 6*d* in 1780: two compotiers, perhaps of the same set, were knocked down at Mr Edkins' sale, in 1875, for the immense sum of 270*l*. "Two beautiful cabinet cups, covers, and stands, antique heads," offer the contrast of 2*l*. 15*s*. in 1780, with 109*l*. in 1874 and 70*l*. in 1875. From the prices realised at other auctions, where private property and private collections were sold, in 1778-1783, we learn that Bristol porcelain was then frequently disposed of at ridiculously low figures—richly decorated pieces not realising more than from 2*s* to 10*s*. each.

Two illustrations (Figs. 42 and 43) represent the most sumptuous varieties of Bristol ware made for the service of the table. The tea-pot has a ground of lapis-lazuli blue, adorned with gilding and surrounding panels of coloured flowers This piece was one of several which had been preserved in the family of W. Cookworthy. it is marked with the Plymouth sign in gold. Nevertheless, we have come to the conclusion (see p. 59) that it was potted and painted at Bristol. The dish-cover and stand (Fig. 43) affords an illustration of the well-known and very usual decoration of Bristol porcelain, the green laurel festoon. This example is in the Jermyn Street collection

Of the commoner or cottage china, made by Champion, there is little to be said. It was thin in substance, and simple and bold in its enamel decoration, which often consisted of a few small scattered bouquets of flowers, with a border of festooned ribbons; in the cups this border occurs on the inside only. The colours, which are roughly laid on, are few, mainly pale blue, lilac, green, and red; no gilding occurs on those pieces. They are very rarely marked, except with the painter's own number. This cottage china was glazed before being fired. Dr. H. P. Blackmore, of Salisbury, has a considerable number of pieces of this kind of Bristol porcelain.

The characteristics of Champion's porcelain may now be given. The first peculiarity which it exhibits (in common with that of Plymouth) consists in the spiral lines or ridges seen upon its surface. The cause has been well explained by Mr. Hugh Owen (*op cit.* p. 311). The paste is milk-white in colour: its fracture is sub-conchoidal and slightly flaky. The lustre of the fractured surfaces is something between greasy and vitreous, under the microscope it is somewhat "hackly." With a high magnifying power the minute rods and granules, called belonites and spherulites respectively (see Chapter I p. 6), are seen in abundance. The hardness of the paste is extraordinarily high, very nearly that of rock crystal, or 7° on the mineralogical scale. The specific gravity of the paste is about 2·37. The colour of the glaze is very faint on the finest specimens, but on the commoner pieces it has a pale bluish tint. It is thin, slightly vesicular or "bubbled," and while smooth is not very shiny, having indeed a rich "creamy" surface. Its hardness approaches 6° and is very nearly that of fused felspar. The cause of the hardness and other fine qualities of Champion's porcelain, is explained when we turn to its analysis. It is to the very high proportion of silica in it that its density, hardness, and durability are mainly due. The larger the proportion of silica present, the higher the temperature the paste will require and will bear in the kiln, and the more compact will be the resulting porcelain. A broken handle of a tea-cup, authenticated as Champion's manufacture, gave, after grinding off the glaze, the following results in 100 parts as the mean of two careful analyses:—

Silica . . 62·92	Lime . . . . 1·28
Alumina . . 33·16	Alkalies . . 2·64

It will be seen that the alkalies and lime of the Bristol porcelain

FIG. 41.—BRISTOL: VASE, PAINTED WITH TREES AND TROPICAL BIRDS.
SCHREIBER COLLECTION.

FIG. 42.—BRISTOL: TEAPOT, RICH BLUE GROUND. SCHREIBER COLLECTION.

FIG. 43.—BRISTOL: COVERED BASKET AND STAND. MUSEUM OF PRACTICAL GEOLOGY.

do not together amount to 4 per cent. This is a remarkably small proportion of fluxing or fusible constituents. The average amount of alkaline oxides in fine Chinese porcelain is 6 per cent; in that of Dresden 6·3. It may be safely affirmed that few, if any, hard porcelains except the Japanese have ever been made with so little alkaline matter as this porcelain of Bristol. And when we study soft English porcelains, we shall often find in them no less than 40 per cent. of bone-earth, alkaline matters, and fluxing salts, associated with no more than 40 per cent. of silica and 20 per cent. of alumina.

It must not be assumed that all Bristol porcelain was identical in composition. Champion specified the use of various proportions of china clay and china stone, ranging from four to sixteen of the former to one of the latter. His glaze also was not always mainly felspathic, but sometimes contained additions which rendered it more fusible.

There are four different marks on Bristol porcelain. The first of these is the alchemic symbol for tin, which was also used at Plymouth. It has been found in one case associated with the characteristic cross of Bristol. It occurs, generally in gold, on very sumptuous vases and other richly decorated pieces, too fine in paste and too perfect in general technique to be accepted as productions of the Plymouth works. The second mark is an imitation of that on Dresden porcelain—the crossed-swords. This occurs in under-glaze blue, except in the case of a few biscuit figures where it is incised in the paste within a triangle also incised: some doubt has, however, been thrown, needlessly we think, upon the attribution of these figures to Bristol. The third mark is the letter B, followed or accompanied by a numeral just as in the case of the fourth mark—a cross. These numbers, which like the B and the cross are in over-glaze enamel colours or in gold, represent the special workman or painter—they range from one to twenty-four. It should be mentioned that a letter *B* and also a cross have been found upon various pieces of earthenware and of soft paste porcelain, which were certainly not made by Champion, but a moment's attention to the character of the material and decoration of such specimens will prevent the possibility of an erroneous conclusion as to their origin.

The word "Bristoll," in relief letters, occurs underneath a few sauce-boats of Bristol manufacture. These pieces are decorated with rather roughly embossed uncoloured festoons of flowers; they are sometimes further decorated with paintings. Mr. H. Willett has a considerable number of sauce-boats of this pattern, some marked as above. In one case the raised mark has been concealed by an enamelled leaf. These pieces are probably of early date.

There is an interesting collection of Champion's china in the Mansion House of the Mayor of Bristol at Clifton. It was presented to the city by Mr. Robert Lang, in the year 1875.

CHAPTER VIII

STAFFORDSHIRE PORCELAIN.

Longton Hall—New Hall—Davenport—Minton—Spode—Wedgwood.

An early manufacture of porcelain was carried on at Longton Hall, in the borough of Stoke-upon-Trent, by William Littler, of Brownhills, near Burslem. His ware seems to have been rather vitreous in character and rather translucent. Two specimens, formerly in the collection of Enoch Wood, now in the Hanley Museum, are authenticated by a descriptive label in the handwriting of their former owner; these, however, are duller in hue than Littler's later productions, and in other respects do not correspond with them: they appear to have been made at least as early as 1752. That Littler's factory was in operation in 1752 is clear from an advertisement in Aris's *Birmingham Gazette*, July 27th of that year, in which notice the public are informed that a large quantity and great variety of very good and fine ornamental porcelain is " now made by William Littler and Co. at Longton Hall, near Newcastle, Staffordshire." How long that manufacture continued we do not know: probably it was soon interrupted by financial difficulties, and then again resumed by Mr. Littler with the assistance of friends or of partners in a new and enlarged venture. Anyhow, an advertisement in Aris's *Birmingham Gazette* of June 20th, 1757, and another in the same journal of June 12th, 1758, conclusively show that the manufacture of porcelain at Longton Hall was then being actively carried on. Of this later manufacture, with which W. Littler's name is associated in all the advertisements, there are, no doubt, many specimens extant. There can be no hesitation in agreeing with Mr. J. E. Nightingale's identification of certain pieces of porcelain in Mr. Franks' collection with the Longton Hall manufacture. They agree, so far as we can judge, with the description of the ware given in the advertisements of 1757 and 1758: and they often bear a very distinctive mark—two L's crossed, with three or four dots underneath—a very appropriate symbol for *Littler, Longton.* This mark resembles the W of Wegeli at Berlin, 1751 The Longton Hall porcelain presents a very close resemblance to a rough kind of Chelsea china. the forms hitherto recognised are chiefly plates and dishes having ornaments and edges of large vine-leaves, embossed and often overlapping. A very rich blue, streaked and flooded or run, is the prevalent and characteristic colour of this porcelain. A delicate scroll-work in opaque white enamel occurs on some pieces—in parts where gold would have been expected if the specimens had been of Chelsea make.

Besides Mr. Franks' specimens of Longton Hall porcelain, other pieces are, or were, in the possession of Mr. J. E Nightingale, the Duchess Dowager of Athole, the Countess of Hopetoun, and Mr. Octavius Morgan. A small, flat-sided octagonal smelling-bottle, with applied flowers and leaves, some almost detached, was exhibited at the Richmond Fine Art Exhibition of 1881; this showed the same quality of streaky blue colour, the same body, and the same general characters as Mr. Franks' marked plates. Quite recently Dr. Diamond has acquired a pair of vases bearing the mark of Longton Hall. They are six and a-quarter inches high by five inches broad, and present all the characteristics of this fabric, the rich streaky blue, the flowers and stalks "in the round," the translucent paste, and those minute signs of a not quite perfect manufacture which one would expect under the circumstances. Each side of these vases bears on a white ground a small spray of delicately painted flowers not at all unlike those commonly found on Chelsea. A pair of vases identical in body, form, and enamelled decoration is in the collection of the author. These pieces, however, unlike Dr. Diamond's specimens, are without any of the rich under-glaze blue colouring, while they are more quaintly adorned with flowers " in the round "—not wreathed about the neck and foot, but stuck singly and upright upon the rim. Our figure 44 gives a fair notion of the style of these curious vases.

Mr. H. Griffith, of Brighton, has several good specimens of Longton Hall porcelain. Amongst them is a small figure group, the only one known. The base of this piece is decorated with applied flowers touched with blue. No doubt many other pieces of this ware are in existence and only await recognition. Commonly, such specimens will have been classed as doubtful or third-rate Chelsea or Bow. Very probably, a fine vase in the Schreiber collection, assigned to Bow, really belongs to Longton.

We may add that the body, or paste, of Littler's porcelain is a vitreous frit similar to that of early Chelsea; bones did not enter into its composition, at least that is the conclusion to which our chemical examination of several specimens has led us.

There are good reasons for believing that Wm. Duesbury, afterwards of Derby, was connected with the Longton porcelain works. He is known to have been residing at Longton Hall in the autumn of 1755. It is probable that the advertisements inserted in the London *Public Advertiser* in April, 1757, relating to an auction sale, by Mr. Ford, of useful and ornamental china made at Longton Hall, relate to productions in which Wm. Duesbury had a hand.

NEW HALL.

The interest attached to the porcelain made at New Hall, Shelton, is due, not to its merits, which are very slight, but to its connection with the labours of Richard Champion, of Bristol

When, in the latter part of the year 1781, Champion finally closed his Bristol factory and left that city, he was engaged in completing the transfer, to a Staffordshire company of potters, of his rights and recipes for hard paste kaolinic porcelain, and, in all probability, of a part, at least, of his appliances. But his skilled enamellers and throwers did not follow their master; and it is impossible to discover in the productions of New Hall any reminiscences of the skill and taste of the Bristol potter. Champion is stated, indeed, by Simeon Shaw and by John Ward to have worked at Tunstall as the manager of a company of potters to whom he had sold his patent, but Mr. Hugh Owen has proved that this statement is incorrect.

Anyhow the New Hall works were not actually in operation until Champion had left Staffordshire for good. They belonged to a firm trading as Hollins, Warburton, and Co, and consisting at first of Samuel Hollins, Jacob Warburton, William Clowes, and Charles Bagnall: John Daniel subsequently became the managing partner. Here hard paste porcelain was introduced into Staffordshire, although soft paste had been made at Longton Hall many years before. The New Hall works were closed in 1825.

In the South Kensington Museum there are two cups and saucers of this porcelain. They are clumsily painted with landscapes in one case, with roughly-drawn figures in the other; they are coarse and crude in effect. A coffee-pot and a bason in the Jermyn Street collection are no better.

Two marks were used at the New Hall works. The earlier, said to have been employed on the hard paste pieces only, was a large incised N; the latter and better-known mark consisted of the name of the factory in italics in a double circle transfer-printed in a dull red or brown. This mark is certainly not confined to the soft paste porcelain made at New Hall after 1820.

DAVENPORT.

In Longport, a suburb of Burslem, John Davenport established a factory for porcelain about the year 1794. The works rapidly became of considerable importance, and produced a large quantity of richly-decorated ware. It is not easy to point out any characters by which Davenport china may be distinguished from that made at the other contemporary factories of Staffordshire; certain small patterns of red, blue and gold, may, in fact, be found alike upon the very similar fine porcelains made by Davenport and by Spode, and at Derby. But the mark of the factory was generally placed upon the pieces; the word Longport, however, when occurring alone cannot be safely assumed to be a mark of the works under discussion. But although other potteries of importance were at work in Longport during the closing years of the last century and the commencement of the present we are not acquainted with any porcelain made in them.

In the South Kensington Museum are three examples of Davenport's china—(339, 399a, and 400 '74). They are ewer-shaped vases, gilt, with flowers painted and in relief. The modelling is not satisfactory, while the general effect is decidedly vulgar.

In the Jermyn Street collection are three specimens of Davenport china. One of these (G 438), a square compotier with gilt scroll-border, is finely painted with a group of fruit. It is probable that the artist was one Thomas Steele, who had been previously employed at the Derby china works.

The marks found on Davenport porcelain are usually printed in over-glaze red or purple, and consist of the name over an anchor or the name with the place of manufacture:

DAVENPORT.   Davenport   DAVENPORT
              LONGPORT.   LONGPORT
                           STAFFORDSHIRE.

One piece in the Jermyn Street collection (G 437) bears the mark painted in red, thus .—Longport.

MINTON

The famous porcelain which bears the name Minton was first made towards the end of the last decade of the last century. Thomas Minton was born at Wyle Cop, Shrewsbury, in 1765. He was apprenticed to Thomas Turner at Caughley, near Broseley, in Shropshire, and then worked for Spode in London. At the age of twenty-three or thereabouts he was established as a master engraver in Staffordshire; he engraved the famous "willow" pattern. Five years afterwards he commenced the manufacture of pottery on a small scale. Not till 1798 is he stated to have begun seriously the production of china, and we should feel disinclined to assign any specimens we have examined to a date earlier than the very close of the last century. The manufacture of porcelain was continued for ten or twelve years, but not on a very large scale. After a cessation of about ten years the making of porcelain was resumed in 1821: the Minton porcelain of the period 1798-1810 is, however, that which is sought for by collectors of old china. Fig. 45 represents a bowl of this period in the South Kensington Museum. It is well potted and of excellent body, into which Cornish china clay and china stone entered. Not unfrequently the decoration exhibits a certain degree of originality of design and refinement of colour not usual in the porcelain of the time. The founder of the works died in 1836. In later times the successors of Thomas Minton have been distinguished for their recognition of the work of Continental ceramic artists. Carrier de Belleuse worked at Minton's, so now does M. L. Solon, whose exquisite low-relief sculptures in *pâte-sur-pâte* (for so they may be called from their manner of production) are unrivalled for delicacy and invention in the domain of ceramic art.

Minton's early mark, which is painted over-glaze, was a direct imitation of that of Sèvres.

A number often accompanies this mark. A later mark, previous, however, to the impressed name MINTON, is an enamelled or gilt ermine spot.

Fig. 44.—LONGTON HALL: VASE WITH RIM OF FLOWERS.
Church Collection.

Fig. 45.—MINTON: BOWL, GILT FOLIAGE ON DARK BLUE GROUND,
PANELS OF FLOWERS. South Kensington Museum. No. 312, '69.

SPODE.

The manufacture of porcelain by Spode, of Stoke, belongs rather to the present century than to the last. To Josiah Spode the younger, son of the first Josiah Spode, who died in 1797, is usually attributed the introduction into the porcelain body of bone ash, the characteristic ingredient of soft English china. But Josiah Spode the younger did not begin making porcelain until some little time after his father's death in 1797, while bone-ash had been in common use at Bow, Chelsea, Worcester, and other china factories for thirty or even forty years previous to that date. Chemical analysis of duly authenticated specimens of these earlier factories proves this statement; not only so, it proves that Spode did not even ascertain for the first time the best proportion of bone-ash to be employed in the porcelain body, quantitative analysis showing that this proportion must have been common knowledge at the time. However, the use of felspar in the china body is, there can be no doubt, an improvement which we owe to the younger Spode. His invention relates to the use of that mineral in a separate form, and not as it occurs in china stone.

Spode's porcelain is distinguished for its mechanical perfection. The potting is excellent, the body uniformly translucent, the glaze smooth, and the gilding solid and rich in tone. The forms and the decorative style of the pieces correspond to the taste of the day, but afford favourable examples of the period. Oriental patterns and embossed work were frequently employed as decorations on Spode porcelain.

In the Jermyn Street collection there are five characteristic examples of this porcelain (G 488, 489 to 491), including a cup and saucer, a pastille burner, a tazza, a vase, and a bottle.

The marks on Spode porcelain are SPODE or Spode, generally printed either in under-glaze blue or over-glaze red or purple, but sometimes impressed in the body; the name is generally accompanied by the number of the pattern. Spode, Felspar Porcelain, in a wreath, also occurs.

WEDGWOOD.

Josiah Wedgwood's jasper ware, though usually ranked with fine stonewares, has many of the characteristics of a hard porcelain, it has been described in Part I. of the present handbook. Wedgwood does not appear to have manufactured porcelain of any of the recognised varieties. But about the year 1805, ten years after Wedgwood's death, his nephew, Thomas Byerley, made a fine true porcelain: it was produced in small quantities for about eight or ten years, and is now but rarely met with. Unfortunately, its style of decoration and the forms it was made to assume do not, in most cases, exhibit a refined taste. The best specimens we have seen were comprised in a richly painted complete dessert service, enamelled with conventional floral designs and richly gilt. Examples of Wedgwood porcelain with painted landscapes, naturalistic flowers, or embossed designs in low relief without colour, will be found in the Jermyn Street collection (G 356 to G 362). There are two specimens (1094 '69 and 1095 '69) in the South Kensington Museum.

The mark on Wedgwood porcelain is almost invariably WEDGWOOD transfer printed in red or (rarely) in blue. Two or three examples of this mark in gold have been noted. The dessert service named in the preceding paragraph bore, in addition to the printed mark, an impressed stamp of three human legs conjoined, like the device of the Isle of Man.

CHAPTER IX

MISCELLANEOUS PORCELAINS.

Lowestoft—Liverpool—Brancas-Lauraguais—Caughley—Coalport—Pinxton —Church Gresley—Rockingham—Nantgarw—Swansea

THE porcelain made during the second half of the eighteenth century at Lowestoft, on the east coast of Suffolk, is not remarkable for any artistic qualities. However, the term "Lowestoft China" has been given, without any warrant, to a vast quantity of hard paste oriental porcelain of inferior character made to order for the English market, and frequently decorated with coats of arms, mottoes, and other designs of European origin. There is no doubt whatever that the mugs with twisted handles, the cups and saucers, and the dinner services of hard paste porcelain which have been attributed to Lowestoft, were neither potted nor painted there. The whole story of many of the above-named services has been well ascertained and entirely negatives any other than a Chinese origin; it is, however, needless to adduce here the evidence which has convinced ceramic connoisseurs of the baselessness of the famous "Lowestoft theory." Here and there we meet, it is true, with bits of Chinese porcelain which have been imported *in the white* and decorated or gilt in England; a few of such pieces may have been painted at Lowestoft—such an admission is all we can safely make. But there is no room to doubt that a soft paste porcelain was made in tolerable quantity at Lowestoft. Of this we have the evidence not merely of contemporary writers but also of signed and dated pieces. According to Gillingham's *History of Lowestoft*, written in 1790, an attempt to manufacture porcelain was there made as early as 1756 by Mr Hewlin Luson, of Gunton Hall, near Lowestoft. In the next year Messrs. Gillingwater, Browne, Aldred, and Rickman succeeded in establishing porcelain works at Lowestoft. In 1770 the firm, Messrs. Robert Browne & Co, had a warehouse in London The factory flourished between 1760 and 1800, but was closed about 1802. The dated pieces are by no means rare, they frequently bear, besides the dates, the name or initials of the persons for whom they were made, and the name of Lowestoft, Yarmouth, or Norwich. The earliest of these pieces heads the following list, the items in which are arranged in chronological sequence.—

1. R.B 1762.
2. ABRM. MOORE, 1765.
3. S C. 1765.
4. Is. Hughes, Sep^{br}. 4th, 1766, Lowestoft.
5. Mic^l. Jaye, Norwich, 1768
6. ELIZATH. BUCKLE, 1768.
7. Edward Morley, 1768.
8. Maria Ann Hoyler, 1770.
9. Ricd. Mason, 1771.
10. James & Mary Curtis, Lowestoft, 1777.
11. Robt. Haward, 1781.
12. S A. Sepr. 26, 1782
13. John Moore, Yarmouth, 1782.
14. J W.S. 1784.
15. G C LOWESTOFT, 1789.

No. 4 of these examples is a remarkable specimen, being painted in black, after the manner of an engraving, with Chinese subjects. It is a large mug, and belongs to Mr. H. Griffith.

No. 5 (in the same collection) is also a mug, having in front, in blue under the glaze, a sun rayed with the disk spotted and representing a face. No. 8 is a large, plain, white flask and bason of considerable size; the name and date, in large characters, are painted underneath both flask and bason. No. 12 is one of three circular ink-pots in Mr. Willett's collection; the others are inscribed in under-glaze blue, "A Trifle from Lowestoft," and "A Trifle from Yarmouth," respectively. No. 13 is a flattened flask belonging to Mr A. W. Franks. A mug crudely painted in colours is in the Willett collection. A large number of other pieces enamelled in colours with roses and other flowers, chequered work and scale patterns, are in existence, and may be assigned to Lowestoft on the evidence furnished by their resemblance to the signed pieces. No factory mark was used at these works.

The paste of Lowestoft porcelain is not so soft as that of Bow or Chelsea. It is slightly yellowish by transmitted light, the glaze being rather bluish and not over bright. There are specks and black spots on most of the pieces, while the blue is of a dull cast. The painting is feeble in drawing, but otherwise reminds one somewhat of the style of St. Cloud porcelain, except where direct imitation of Chinese design has been attempted.

LIVERPOOL.

The colony of workmen from the Staffordshire potteries which had settled at "Herculaneum" on the south side of the Mersey, near Liverpool, was engaged chiefly in the manufacture of earthenware. But about the year 1800 porcelain was there produced. Some of this was decorated with flowers and birds in enamel associated with rich gilding; transfer-printing in black and colours was also employed at these works on porcelain as well as on earthenware. In the Jermyn Street collection there is a cup and saucer (S. 5) which, though unmarked, may be safely assigned to Herculaneum; this word impressed or transfer-printed occurs on some pieces of this porcelain.

But in Liverpool itself three potters produced porcelain long before the establishment of the Herculaneum works. One of these was R. Chaffers; another, Christian by name, seems to have made a vitreous porcellanous frit as early as 1769 at least. Seth Pennington, of Shaw's Brow, Liverpool, was also at work about the same time. From the recipe for "china body," which was given by Pennington, March 18th, 1769, we may calculate its constitutents per one hundred parts as follows: —

Bone-ash	33·3
Lynn sand	22·2
Flint	19·5
Clay	25·0

The first three ingredients were to be fritted together and the clay afterwards added. The nature of the clay is not specified, but at that time Cornish china-clay had been made known through Cookworthy's patent. The use of bone-ash also must then have been familiar on account of its employment at Bow, Chelsea, and Worcester.

We know next to nothing of the productions of Seth Pennington. His pieces are said to have been marked with a P in blue under the glaze; they are also stated to have been conspicuous for a particularly beautiful blue colour.

Some vases and beakers of oriental form, and marked with the supposed sign of Pennington's china, have been from time to time observed. They much resemble what may be called the cottage china, painted under the glaze in blue, which was made at Worcester and at Caughley. But until such pieces have been identified with the productions of the Liverpool factory further description would be useless. The two specimens (6788 '60 and 725 '53) of so-called Liverpool porcelain in the South Kensington Museum, a transfer-printed mug, and a plate with a pierced border of basket-work and painted in colours, cannot with certainty be given to Liverpool. But in the Willett collection there is a quart mug which not only bears amongst its ornaments representations of the bird called the "liver," but the words FREDERICK HEINZELMAN—LIVERPOOL, and the date 1799; it may be safely attributed to one of the Liverpool factories. A tea-service of Liverpool porcelain with transfer-printing in black was recently sold at Christies'; it was catalogued as Worcester. Very probably it was made by Chaffers.

BRANCAS-LAURAGUAIS.

Some objection may be raised to the inclusion of the hard porcelain of the Comte de Brancas-Lauraguais amongst English ceramic productions. But the English patent taken out by the Count, his sojourn in England, his known acquaintance with Cornish kaolin, the incidental allusions to his discoveries in contemporary literature, and the peculiarities of those of his productions which have been lately found in this country, point to one conclusion, namely, that he made and decorated hard kaolinic porcelain in this country as well as in his own. He began his ceramic career by discovering the kaolin of Alençon about the year 1758. He worked at Sèvres, and very probably at Chelsea also. His English patent for hard or true china was taken out on June 10th, 1766, but his invention was never specified. Thus he anticipated W. Cookworthy's patent by nearly two years. Brancas-Lauraguais and his porcelain are named in the *Scot's* magazine for 1764, by Dr. Erasmus Darwin in a letter (April 1766) to Josiah Wedgwood; and by the Abbé Raynal. Horace Walpole possessed a porcelain reproduction, by the Count, of the Bacchus of Michael Angelo. In M. Gasnault's collection there is a medallion dated "Octobre, 1764." The Rouen Museum possesses a specimen bearing the date "Septembre, 1768." The Musée Céramique of Sèvres has no less than three pieces of Brancas-Lauraguais porcelain. M. Jules Vallet has a plate with coloured decoration of oriental character. The late M Jacquemart owned a cup. There were three specimens in the Alexandra Palace loan collection; these were destroyed in the disastrous fire of June 1873. One of these last-named pieces was a tea-bottle of angular form with rounded shoulders; its decoration of flowers was entirely in the Chelsea style of the second period. The paste of this specimen was fine, hard, and of good colour; altogether this piece showed to what a high degree of excellence the Count had carried his invention; it was marked in purple enamel with a cursive B and L conjoined. The other specimens in the same exhibition were two spirally-fluted columns with bands of enamel flowers winding up the hollows. One of these was marked with the above described monogram in black, the other in purplish-brown. A fragmentary column of the same set was submitted to chemical analysis. It gave in 100 parts:—

Silica 58	Lime 1
Alumina . . . 36	Potash 3
Oxide of Iron . . 1	Soda 1

The kaolinic character of this ware is evident from the above numbers. The specific gravity of the fragment analysed was 2.531.

CAUGHLEY.—1772-1799.

Although the potworks of Caughley, near Broseley, in Shropshire, were established as early as 1754, we know next to nothing of their productions until Thomas Turner had come from Worcester, in 1772, and had introduced a superior quality of porcelain and a rich deep blue colour for under-glaze printing. Chinese subjects are frequently found upon Caughley porcelain belonging to this "Turner" period. Many of the finer and more highly decorated pieces made at this time cannot be distinguished from the contemporaneous or perhaps somewhat earlier productions of the Worcester works. For instance, in the Bond collection, sold at

Fig. 46.—CAUGHLEY: SUGAR BASON AND COVER. Museum of Practical Geology.

Fig. 47.—PINXTON: ICE-PAIL, CANARY-YELLOW GROUND WITH FLORAL BORDER. South Kensington Museum. No. 308, '69.

Leeds in October 1884, there was a very richly enamelled cup and saucer, painted with flowers which would have done no discredit to the best potter and best artist of Worcester; it was, however, marked with the S of Caughley. It brought at the above sale no less a price than seven guineas. On the same occasion four oval baskets, covers, and stands were sold, some marked with an S and others with a C: these would have been generally attributed to Worcester if unmarked. They were of basket-work, with small four-petaled flowers at the intersections of the lattice, and they were further decorated with raised blossoms, and touches of under-glaze blue. A similar piece is 3261 '53 in the South Kensington Museum, but this bears the perplexing marks of a Y and an L, and is freely, though rather roughly, decorated with enamel colours. It has not hitherto been assigned to any particular English factory.

The marks used at Caughley from 1772 until 1799 were, we believe, an S or a C printed or painted in under-glaze blue; a crescent, filled in entirely with blue, has been assigned to these works on insufficient grounds—certainly it was used at Worcester. The word SALOPIAN impresssd in the paste belongs to Caughley.

A few years after the commencement of the second period of the Caughley factory rich gilding was successfully introduced. A favourable example of porcelain so decorated is the covered sugar-bason in the Jermyn Street collection, shown in Fig. 46. It has a ribbed body divided into compartments by vertical lines and ornamented with flowers in a rich under-glaze blue and in gold: the mark is in under-glaze blue. Other specimens in the same collection include cups and saucers, mugs, jugs, dessert-plates and dishes, for the most part decorated with under-glaze printing in blue. Some of these pieces are marked with disguised Arabic numerals so associated with casual strokes and flourishes as to resemble Chinese signs. These curious marks occur also on Dutch delft made in the first half of the eighteenth century; it is likely that from this source Caughley,

Bow, and Worcester took the idea. It is, indeed, a matter of some difficulty to determine to which of these three factories pieces so marked belong. The underglaze-printed Caughley porcelain is like the commoner similar ware made at Worcester, while the painted and gilt pieces resemble in style the earlier crown-Derby productions.

In the South Kensington Museum there are but five examples of Caughley porcelain, one the basket already named, the others (350 '54; 680 to 680*b* '75) are blue printed cups of poor quality.

The Caughley works were purchased by John Rose of Coalport, in 1799; they were closed in 1814.

COALPORT.

Mr. John Rose was apprenticed to Thomas Turner of Caughley, but about the year 1780 he commenced a pottery on his own account at Jackfield, a place in the neighbourhood, which had formerly been famous for its productions in common earthenware. Not long after Rose's establishment at Jackfield had been opened he removed it to Coalport on the opposite side of the Severn. In 1799, on the death of Turner, he purchased the Caughley works, which he carried on until 1814 when he abandoned them, removing the business to his factory at Coalport. Rose occasionally decorated the white porcelain of other factories. In 1841 he died, but the works, known sometimes as Coalbrookdale, are still carried on. John Rose obtained, in the year 1820, a gold medal from the Society of Arts for a glaze containing neither lead nor arsenic. It was compounded of—

Felspar	27 parts	Cornish china clay	3 parts
Borax	18 ,,	Nitre	3 ,,
Lynn sand	4 ,,	Soda	3 ,,

This mixture was fritted, and three parts of calcined borax then added.

Of the later productions of Coalport there are several characteristic examples in the Jermyn Street collection. The vases are often coarse imitations of Chelsea porcelain, and sometimes bear what must be looked upon as the forged mark of an anchor in gold. Cups and saucers are also found having two L's crossed, in imitation of Sèvres; marks of other factories, English and foreign, are also found upon pieces of Coalport porcelain and earthenware. Besides imitative marks the following are found upon the later Coalport productions:—

Coalport   JOHN ROSE & CO.   C B D.
            COLEBROOKDALE.

The name of Messrs. Daniell of London occurs on some pieces of Coalport porcelain.

PINXTON.

The porcelain works at Pinxton, established about the year 1795 by Mr. John Coke, appear to have owed much to a skilful flower-painter and practical potter who had been previously employed both at Derby and Worcester. William Billingsley, "Beely," is known to have been engaged at Derby before the founding of the Pinxton factory; in 1800 he left Pinxton to work successively at Mansfield, Torksey, Worcester, Nantgarw, Swansea, and Coalport. The quality of the Pinxton porcelain deteriorated after Billingsley left the works there. The body or paste was coarser and less translucent, while the decoration was cruder in colour and more roughly drawn. Instead of flowers, festoons and sprigs, landscapes in panels formed the chief decorations of the more costly pieces produced at the works. In the Jermyn Street collection the dessert dish (J 95) is an example of the later and inferior time. Two ice-pails in the South Kensington Museum (308, 309 '69) were probably decorated by Billingsley, they are important pieces of fine quality The bodies are coloured of a deep primrose yellow on which are scrolls of pencilled grey. A border of well-painted flowers on a greyish ground encircles the upper part. One of these ice-pails is shown in Fig 47. The works were closed in 1812. A cursive P painted in red over the glaze is the only mark which has been identified as belonging exclusively to the Pinxton factory.

CHURCH GRESLEY.—1795-1808.

At Church Gresley, in Leicestershire, a porcelain factory was founded by Sir Nigel Gresley in the year 1795. He built his china-works close to his residence, Gresley Hall. His workmen came from the Staffordshire potteries; W. Coffee, of Derby, the modeller, assisted him during the summer of 1795. He obtained clay from Devonshire and Cornwall. Breakfast, dinner, dessert, and tea services were made at the works as well as small figures of dogs, birds, &c. Much attention was paid to the painting and gilding of the pieces, the best artists that could be obtained being secured by the owner of the works. A favourite pattern for the plates was a tree in blue with carefully painted birds upon the branches. Owing to heavy losses Sir Nigel Gresley ceded the factory, in 1800, to Mr William Nadin, a colliery owner of the neighbourhood. Under their new proprietor the china works were continued for four or five years without pecuniary success, and were then carried on by a company, which became bankrupt in 1808. The "china house" was then for the most part pulled down. The warping of the pieces during firing seems never to have been overcome in these works; oven after oven was drawn, and the plates found to be of all shapes but the right one. On one occasion Mr. Nadin received an order from Queen Charlotte through her Majesty's Deputy-Chamberlain, Colonel Desborough, for "the handsomest dinner service he could make" regardless of price, but the order was never executed. As yet no pieces of Church Gresley porcelain, identified with perfect certainty, are in any public collection, unless those in Jermyn Street may prove authentic. It is worth while, however, to describe these six specimens with some minuteness, as thereby attention may be drawn to this obscure factory and further light thrown upon its productions The six pieces referred to belong to two distinct breakfast services—a tea-cup, a coffee-cup, and a saucer of each set. The paste of one set is thin, white, and translucent; the gilding is good, but the enamel-painting of landscapes and buildings in medallions very poor and inartistic. The paste of the pieces belonging to the other set is less translucent, showing also grey specks and other signs of an imperfect manufacture. These pieces, moreover, though gilt in the same style as the previously-named specimens, are decorated with small coarsely-painted groups of flowers inclosed in a kind of lattice-work of gilt bands; a good canary-yellow, similar to that on some Derby porcelain, is also introduced in small spaces between some of the gilt stripes. All the above pieces would be regarded by collectors as resembling inferior Derby china of late date, but there are some reasons for considering them as likely to have been made at Church Gresley.

ROCKINGHAM.

The various kinds of earthenware made at Swinton, near Rotherham, Yorkshire, and known as Rockingham ware, have been named in the *Handbook of English Earthenware*, pp. 105 to 107. The manufacture of porcelain was not attempted at these works until the year 1820 or thereabout, a period which does not fall within the immediate scope of the present handbook. A few words of description may, however, be here given, particularly as the manufacture was discontinued in 1842 and no lengthy account of it is needed.

Technically the body, the potting, the glazing, the gilding, and the enamelling of Rockingham porcelain were of marked excellence; very large pieces were also produced with success at the works, as, for example, the vase and cover in the South Kensington Museum (No. 47 '69), which, together, measure no less than three feet two and a-half inches in height.[1] But the artistic qualities of Rockingham porcelain cannot generally be regarded as worthy of commendation. The forms adopted for the ornamental pieces were often ungainly, the painting lifeless, and the gilding lavish. The specimens in the Jermyn Street collection (M 1 to M 10) include vases, plates, cups and saucers, and figures. Busts, spill-vases, and flower-baskets were also made at the Rockingham works; the former, as well as the statuettes, being sometimes of unglazed porcelain-biscuit, similar to the biscuit of Derby. Two biscuit groups, of a boy with a rabbit and a girl with a lamb, are in the Willett collection. They are marked with the Griffin crest, and ROCKINGHAM WORKS, BRAMELD & Co. No. 44—all impressed in the paste. The glazed pieces are usually marked in the same way, but in transfer-printing; sometimes under the griffin we find the words "Rockingham" and "Brameld," or one or other of these alone. It is believed that the griffin crest was not used as a mark until the year 1826, when Earl Fitzwilliam rendered some pecuniary assistance to the manufacturers.

In the Jermyn Street collection there are several pieces of Rockingham porcelain marked with this crest, and below it various modifications of the above-mentioned names, all transfer-printed in red or purple. Amongst these varieties of the mark may be found—

Rockingham Works,
Brameld
Manufacturer to the King.

Royal Rock^m Works,
Brameld.

Rockingham Works,
Brameld

A particularly fine collection of Rockingham porcelain was dispersed at Leeds in October 1884. The owner, Mr. Edward

[1] The flower-painting on this immense vase is of extraordinary fineness as to drawing and richness of colour.

Bond, had secured some of these pieces many years ago, not long after the closing of the works. The prices realised at the sale were in some cases very large. Four pattern plates, richly enamelled and gilt, brought together no less than 101 guineas. Three of these pieces bore the Royal Arms of England in the centre; the fourth had an exquisitely finished picture of a group of mushrooms. A breakfast service, of forty-one pieces, reminded one at once of Worcester and of Sèvres. It had a powder-blue border with coloured flowers and gilt leaves in sprays symmetrically arranged. It was sold for thirty-one guineas. Two large, but badly moulded, hexagonal vases were in the same collection. A handsome bowl, cover, and stand, incrusted with coloured flowers in full relief, brought twenty-two guineas. For thirteen and a-half guineas a remarkable triumph of the potter's art was sold—a basket and cover wholly constructed of delicate porcelain straws; this piece was also incrusted with flowers.

NANTGARW.

At Nantgarw, nine miles north of Cardiff, a small porcelain factory was established about the year 1811. Samuel Walker and William Billingsley ("Beely") who had been in the employment of Messrs. Flight and Barr of Worcester, started this small factory at Nantgarw, where they made a soft and glassy but very beautiful translucent porcelain. The decorations of the ware consisted mainly of painted flowers and birds with gilding. Plates, dishes, and teaware (chiefly cups and saucers) were made in considerable quantity; vases were rarely attempted. The pieces were almost invariably marked with the name of the place NANT-GARW and the initials C.W impressed in the paste. C.W. These initials most probably are intended to stand for China Works. Arrangements for removing the small

Nantgarw works to the Cambrian Pottery at Swansea seem to have been partially carried out about the year 1814 or 1815, but they were never completed. Billingsley remained at Nantgarw from 1811 till 1814, when he went to Swansea. He returned in 1817, but two years afterwards, until his death in 1828, was at work for John Rose at Coalport. It appears that another manufactory of china was carried on at Nantgarw after Billingsley's removal in 1819, but the productions of its proprietor, W. W. Young, have not as yet been identified.

There are twelve specimens of Nantgarw porcelain in the Jermyn Street collection (Q 1 to 12). Of these 2, 4, 6, all plates, illustrate to advantage the exquisite paste and delicate flower-painting for which both Swansea and Nantgarw were famous. In the South Kensington Museum are examples belonging to the Schreiber collection. Four-and twenty fine pieces of this porcelain were destroyed in the Alexandra Palace fire. Among the South Kensington specimens are two cups and saucers (706, 706a '68) decorated in the style of some of the late Worcester pieces, Fig 48. On these there is a carefully painted lilac and gold scale-ground with reserved white panels of butterflies and tropical birds; despite the delicate finish of the painting the effect is hard, poor, and cold.

SWANSEA

The remarkable translucent porcelain made at the Swansea factory seems to have originated from the communications established betwen Walker and Billingsley of Nantgarw, and Mr. L. W. Dillwyn of the Cambrian Pottery. The description, given on p. 93, of the paste and decoration of Nantgarw porcelain is almost equally applicable to the productions of the Swansea works. The delicately and deftly painted roses of Billingsley occur on both fabrics, but certain embossed patterns in low

FIG. 48.—NANTGARW: SAUCER, LILAC AND GILT SCALE GROUND, PANELS OF INSECTS AND BIRDS. SOUTH KENSINGTON MUSEUM. No. 706, '68.

FIG. 49.—SWANSEA: COFFEE-CAN. SOUTH KENSINGTON MUSEUM. No. 197, '78.

relief and uncoloured are almost characteristic of Swansea This porcelain, however, is frequently found having for decoration some of those beautiful and faithful transcripts from natural history objects, which were painted by W. W. Young, the draughtsman employed by Mr. Dillwyn. Flowers, generally a single spray of one kind only, and of the natural size, commonly occur on plates and dishes of Swansea porcelain. In some cases these have their outlines and shading in transfer-printing, the enamel colours being laid on subsequently by hand in broad washes.

The manufacture of porcelain at Swansea by Billingsley and Walker ceased in 1817 In that year the partnership of L. W Dillwyn with the Bevingtons was dissolved. The making of porcelain ended in 1824, if not before. Cornish china-clay, china-stone, and steatite and glass were used for the paste.

The marks on Swansea porcelain are—SWANSEA impressed, sometimes with a trident, SWANSEA, and sometimes enamelled

in red in a script character—*Swansea*.

There is a breakfast service of this porcelain in the South Kensington Museum (107 to 107 J. 1878). It is decorated with dog-roses and other wild flowers fairly painted, and with gilding (see Fig. 49). The ten pieces cost 14*l*. In the Jermyn Street collection there are twelve specimens (P 20 to P 31); twenty-seven examples were destroyed in the Alexandra Palace fire; some of these had transfer-printed landscapes or figures; some were decorated with copper and platinum lustre.

Biscuit porcelain of good quality was made at the Swansea works. There is a small specimen of this kind in Jermyn Street—a figure of a ram couchant. The impressed mark on the base is peculiar, BEVINGTON & CO. with the letters I W. When SWANSEA porcelain bears the above mark it belongs to the period 1817—1824, when the new firm of T. and J. Bevington & Co carried on the factory.

INDEX.

	PAGE
ALUMINA in clay	3
Alumina in porcelain	2
Analyses of porcelain . 21, 29, 70,	87
Anchor and Dagger mark	33
Anchor as Chelsea mark	24
Anchor in Davenport mark	77
Animals in Chelsea porcelain	24
Armorial Bristol plaques	67
Armorial china	81
B and L conjoined, a mark	86
B, a mark on porcelain	30, 71
Baskets of Caughley porcelain	87
Bevington & Co, of Swansea	95
Billingsley, W., painter . 39, 89,	93
Binns, R W , of Worcester	43, 51
Biscuit, Derby	40, 41
Biscuit, Bristol	67
Bloor, R , of Derby	37
Blue on Worcester porcelain	50
Body of porcelain	7
Bond collection	87, 93
Bone-ash . . 2, 4, 21, 79,	84
Bone-ash at Worcester	54
Bones used first at Bow	29
Bones in porcelain	7, 79
Bottger	5
Bow marks	30
Bow patterns	28
Bow sales	27
Bow works	27
Brameld & Co.	92
Brancas-Lauraguais porcelain	5, 85
Bristol flower-plaques	67
Bristol factory	57
Bristol marks	61, 71
Bristol porcelain infusible	67

	PAGE
Bristol porcelain sales	63
Bristol portrait medallions	66
Bristol vases .	65, 68
Bristoll, as mark	72
Browne, R. & Co., Lowestoft	82
Burke's tea-service	66
Butter boats	72
CAMELFORD, Lord	57
Caughley porcelain	50, 86
Cement in porcelain	7
Chamberlains of Worcester	53
Champion, R , of Bristol	62
Champion's apprentices	65
Champion's death	67
Champion's last statuette	66
Champion's recipes	71
Chelsea auctions	16, 19
Chelsea-Derby	23, 38, 39
Chelsea enamel-colours	17, 19
Chelsea porcelain analysed	21
Chelsea scent-bottles	17, 22
Chelsea works	14, 16
Chelsea works sold	19
China-clay	2, 3, 5, 56
China called Lowestoft	81
China-stone	3, 56
Chinese designs	12, 45, 49, 50
Church Gresley porcelain	90
Classification of porcelains	6, 7
Coalport porcelain	88
Colebrookdale porcelain	89
Cookworthy, W , of Plymouth	6, 56
Cookworthy's patent	57, 65
Cottage-china of Bristol	65, 69
Cottage-china of Liverpool	84
Craft, T , his bowl	27

INDEX.

	PAGE
Crescent marks	52
Cross, mark on Bristol	72
Crowther, J., of Bow	26
Crowther, R., on a plate	26
DAVENPORT porcelain	77
Davis, W., of Worcester	43
Decadence of English porcelain	11, 75, 92
Derby, Chelsea	23, 36, 38
Derby frit	42
Derby marks	37, 38
Derby porcelain works	35
Derby sales	36, 41
Derby statuettes	40
Diamond, Dr. H. W., collection	21, 25, 74
Diana, Derby figure	40
Dillwyn, L. W., of Swansea	94
Donaldson, of Worcester	49
Dresden mark	40, 53, 71
Duesbury, W., of Derby	19, 27, 37
Duesbury family	37
EARLY Chelsea-paste	20, 21
Ermine-spot as a mark	79
FALSTAFF figures	18
Faults of English porcelain	11, 12
Felspar	3
Felspar in porcelain	79
Figures of Worcester porcelain	54
Flight, T.	45, 53
Flight and Barr	53
Fogo, C. C., painter	49
Forged marks	64, 89
Franks, A. W., collection	17, 74
Frederick the Great	47
French porcelain	4
Frye, T., of Bow	26, 29, 33
GILDING on Chelsea porcelain	21, 23
Giles's kiln	28, 49
Gillingwater & Co.	82
Glass in porcelain	7, 29, 53
Glaze of porcelain	7, 54, 70
Glaze without lead	88
Goat milk-jugs	33, 34
Gouyn, C., of Chelsea	14
Granby, Marquis of	74

	PAGE
Gresley, Sir Nigel	90
Griffin as a mark	92
Griffith, H. collection	75, 82
HANCOCK, R., of Worcester	47
Harlequin, figure of	19
Haslem, J., of Derby	38
Heylyn, E., of Bow	26
Holdship, R. & J.	43, 47
Hollins & Co.	76
IMITATIVE Chinese marks	87
Imitative porcelain	10
Impressed patterns	51
Italian porcelain	4
JAPAN patterns	42
Jet-enamelled china	46
KAOLIN	2, 3, 5, 56
MARKS on porcelain, 22, 24, 25, 33, 37, 52, 60, 71, 74, 77, 78, 89, 92, 93, 95	
Medici porcelain	4
Meissen porcelain	5
Minton porcelain	78
Minton, T.	78
NADIN, W.	90
Nantgarw porcelain	93
Nightingale, J. E., his researches	22, 64, 74
Nightingale, J. E., his collection	51, 74
ORIGINALITY of English porcelain	11
Oriental porcelain painted at Bow	9
O'Neale, painter	49
PARTRIDGE pattern	31
Patents for porcelain	28, 57, 65
Phosphoric acid in porcelain	21
Pinxton porcelain	89

INDEX.

	PAGE
Planché, A., of Derby	35
Plants in Chelsea porcelain	24
Plymouth body	60
Plymouth delft	60
Plymouth glaze	59
Plymouth marks	58, 60, 69
Plymouth porcelain	56
Porcelain, classification of	7, 8
Porcelain, hard and soft	8
Porcelain in China	1
Porcelain mounted	2
Porcelain sent to Europe	2
Porcelain, so called, of Dwight	9
"Potteries" district	11
Prices of Bristol porcelain	68
Prices of Chelsea porcelain	20, 23, 24
Prices of Worcester porcelain	54
Printing and painting combined	47
Printing over-glaze	46
Printing under-glaze	46
Productions of Bow, Chelsea, and Worcester	22, 32, 51
Prunus flower on porcelain	31
Quail and Wheatsheaf pattern	31
Rockingham porcelain	91
Rococo Chelsea vases	22
Rose, J., of Coalport	88, 94
Salopian porcelain	87
Seasons, Bristol figures	68
Sèvres, enamel colours	17
Shell centrepieces	28, 50
Smith tea-service	66
Soapstone	2, 3, 53
Soapy rock	2, 3, 53
Soft porcelain	3, 7

	PAGE
Spiral ridges on porcelain	70
Spode porcelain	79
Sprimont, N., of Chelsea	14, 15
Steatite in porcelain	53
Steele, T., painter	77
Stephens, W., of Bristol	65
Swansea marks	95
Swansea porcelain	94
Tea-services of Bristol	66
Tebo, modeller	68
Tobacco bowl	55
Unaker or china-clay	26, 29, 54
Venice porcelain	4
W, Worcester mark	52
Walker, G., painter	93
Wall, Dr. J., of Worcester	43
Wedgwood opposes Champion	65
Wedgwood porcelain	80
Willett, H., collection	18, 82
Worcester colours	48
Worcester, its decadence	45
Worcester influenced by Chelsea	49
Worcester marks	52
Worcester porcelain	43
Worcester porcelain, prices of	54
Worcester works, changes in	45
Worcester works, site of	44
Xhrouet of Sèvres	18
Young, W. W., Swansea painter	95

THE END

UNIVERSITY OF CALIFORNIA LIBRARY, LOS ANGELES

This book is DUE on the last date stamped below.

UCLA
ART LIBRARY

MAY 6 1993

Phone Renewals
310/825-9188

UCLA-Art Library
NK 4485 C47e

L 006 227 369 3

UC SOUTHERN REGIONAL LIBRARY FACILITY

AA 000 784 040 8

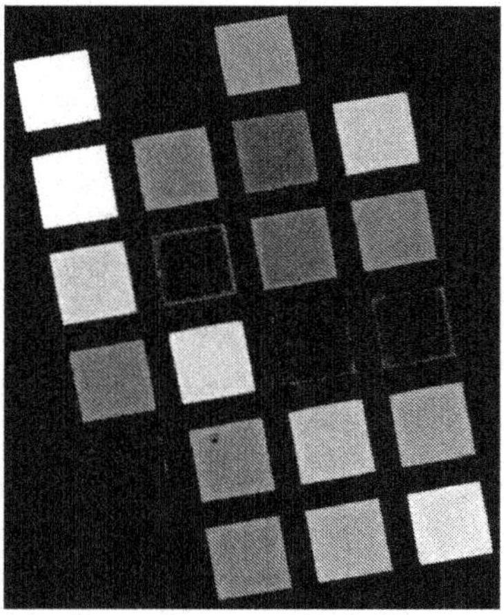